Using Microsoft® Windows 3.1

Using Microsoft® Windows 3.1

Jerry Horazdovsky, Ph.D.

Anoka-Ramsey Community College

HOUGHTON MIFFLIN COMPANY   Boston   Toronto

Geneva, Illinois   Palo Alto   Princeton, New Jersey

Senior Sponsoring Editor: Donald J. Golini
Development Editor: Erika Desuk/Joanne Dauksewicz
Senior Project Editor: Toni Haluga
Editorial Assistant: Tracy Theriault
Production/Design Coordinator: Caroline Ryan
Senior Manufacturing Coordinator: Priscilla Bailey
Marketing Manager: Robert Wolcott

ISBN: 0-395-66037-8

123456789-CW-97 96 95 94 93

Contents

6   Desktop Accessories   125

Preface

Using Microsoft Windows 3.1 is designed to quickly give beginning and experienced computer users a solid working knowledge of Windows. The materials cover *fundamental* Windows concepts, techniques, and standard operating procedures. Windows is very powerful and very flexible. This book does not attempt to discuss every Windows activity or all the ways one task can be accomplished. However, reading the chapters and completing the exercises and applications will help you to become an efficient Windows user.

The chapters are designed to ensure rapid mastery of the topics. A typical chapter consists of:

- Explanations and illustrations of Windows concepts and procedures as well as reasons for knowing the information.

- Step-by-step, hands-on exercises for practicing Windows procedures. (Each step number is enclosed in a box to indicate that the activity should be completed on the user's computer.)

- Additional tips and notes that point out helpful procedures or warn of dangerous situations.

- End-of-chapter summaries that review key concepts and commands.

- End-of-chapter applications that allow readers to test and reinforce their knowledge. (Readers will need access to Windows 3.1, a copy of the *Using Windows 3.1 Data Disk,* and one additional blank disk, to complete the exercises and applications.)

Chapter 1 examines some of the basic skills needed to operate in the Windows graphical environment. The information and instructions presented throughout the text are based on certain assumptions about the reader and the computer equipment being used. These assumptions include:

1. Windows has been properly installed on the computer's hard drive or file server. (Appendix A discusses the Windows installation procedure.)

2. The computer meets or exceeds the minimum Windows 3.1 hardware requirements. (Appendix A also lists the minimum computer hardware requirements.)

3. Although the keyboard may be used to complete the Windows commands, most people use the mouse to execute the majority of Windows activities. Therefore, the mouse movements are listed for each Windows activity discussed in the text. When appropriate, keyboard commands are also given.

4. The "typical" Windows user needs to learn a fundamental core of Windows commands and procedures. This text explains how to complete these fundamental activities. The text does not include coverage of commands or functions that require special computer hardware, change the Windows installation files, or alter the standard operation of the Windows package. The Windows manuals and the Windows Help facility provide additional information in these areas.

5. Most users install Windows on the C: drive (normally configured as the hard disk drive) of the computer system. To serve the largest group of Windows users, all explanations and directions are written with the assumption that the C: drive is designated for holding the Windows package and that the *Using Microsoft Windows 3.1* Data Disk is placed in the A: drive. If this configuration does not reflect your setup (i.e., you are running Windows from a network drive), simply write the proper drive letter above the letter in the text.

In addition to the ten chapters covering basic Windows content, two appendices explain additional materials that many users will find helpful.

Acknowledgments

This book could not have been completed without the help of certain key individuals. The author gratefully acknowledges the efforts received from Jack IntVeld, David Strand, the students of Anoka-Ramsey Community College, and Erika Desuk and Raymond Deveaux from Houghton Mifflin Company. A special thank you goes to Patty, Josie, Earl, and Lil Horazdovsky for all the support, patience, and understanding given to me during the writing of this book.

In addition I would like to thank the following reviewers for their special assistance: Ron Goodman, *Quincy College;* Dan Harper, *Stautzenberger College;* Dr. Margaret Jamison, *Ferrum College;* Professor Mike Michaelson, *Palomar College;* Barbara J. Minnick, *Indiana State University;* Dr. Patsy Nichols, *Murray State University;* Robert E. Norton, *San Diego State University;* and Professor Seymour J. Wolfson, *Wayne State University.*

1

Welcome to Windows

Working with the Microsoft Windows graphical computing environment has helped millions of people become more effective computer users. Windows provides a friendly on-screen setting consisting of numerous easy-to-use graphic images and drop-down lists of commands. The typical Windows user communicates with the computer through the use of a pointing device, such as a mouse. When the user points (and clicks) on an image or phrase displayed on the screen, the computer executes a corresponding activity. For example, to start a software program, the user merely points to the program symbol on the Windows screen and presses the mouse button.

Windows works with the disk operating system (DOS) to provide this new environment. The typical single-line DOS prompt (i.e., C:\>) is replaced with a full-screen graphical user interface (GUI—pronounced "gooey") consisting of the numerous images and lists of commands. Because working in the Windows environment eliminates the need for memorizing various DOS character commands (such as DIR, REN, and FORMAT), many computer users feel it is easier to control their computing activities from the graphical environment than from the traditional DOS setting.

Windows has become so popular that many companies that sell microcomputers place a copy of

Windows on every computer they sell. The popularity of Windows stems from its ease of use and the power it gives the user. Along with providing access to the graphical environment, additional reasons for learning to use Windows include:

- Gaining the ability to conduct numerous computing activities (i.e., word processing spellchecking, spreadsheet printing, and database searching) at the same time.

- Developing a consistent method for working with a wide variety of computer applications.

- Easily linking and transferring data from different applications into one document.

- Making more efficient use of computer memory to allow for running today's larger, more complex software programs.

- Customizing the computing environment to fit your computing style.

Basic Terminology and Window Elements

The first time you start Windows, your monitor screen may look similar to the illustrated display shown in Figure 1.1.

NOTE: Displays on your monitor may not exactly match the screens shown in this text. Don't worry about slight differences in appearance. You will soon learn how to customize the look of your Windows screens.

Descriptions of the various elements identified in Figure 1.1 are listed below.

Windows: this term has a double meaning in this text. When the first letter is capitalized, the term normally refers to the Microsoft Windows environment. When the term appears in lowercase letters, it refers to a rectangular region on the screen.

Window borders: the four sets of double lines that comprise the perimeter of the window. The size of the rectangular window can usually be changed by adjusting its borders.

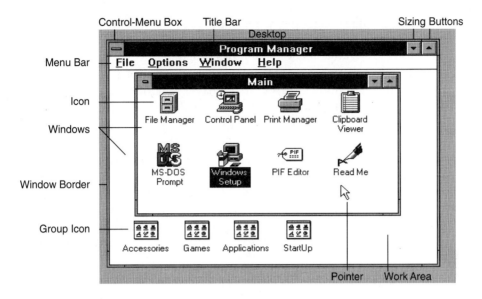

Figure 1.1 The Program Manager window containing the Main group window.

Desktop: the screen background upon which the windows appear.

Control-menu box: the small, square box containing a dash, located in the upper-left corner of the window. It is used for closing the window or displaying the Control menu.

Title bar: the narrow area located directly below the window's top border that includes the name of the window.

Sizing buttons: the small boxes (shaded to appear three-dimensional) immediately to the right of the title bar.

1. **Minimize button:** The button, containing a down arrow, that is used for reducing a window to an icon (see the term "icons" listed below).

2. **Maximize button:** The button, containing an up arrow, that is used for enlarging the window to fill either the entire desktop, or the space within the program window in which the current window resides.

3. **Restore button:** (not shown in Figure 1.1) The button, containing an up and down arrow, that is displayed only when a window is maximized. It is used for returning a maximized window to its previous size and location on the desktop.

Icons: graphic images (or symbols) used to represent many windows elements, such as disk drivers, applications, or documents. Icons may be used to start many of the Windows programs.

Group Icon: an icon representing a collection of applications, accessories, or documents within the Program Manager window.

Menu bar: the line of words below the title bar. A menu bar provides access to lists of commands that may be executed at a particular point in the program.

Work area: the area inside of a window where data is entered.

Pointer: the indicator (often displayed as a slanted upward-pointing arrow) that shows the area of the screen that will be affected when the mouse button is pressed. The pointer moves when the mouse is moved. The shape of the pointer changes depending upon its location within particular windows. (Also referred to as the mouse pointer or screen pointer.)

Working with Windows

Although it contains a multitude of features, Windows is easy to use, once you know a few of its basic concepts. Completing the following sections will provide the foundation needed to use the variety of applications and accessories in the Windows software package. The standard operations of other Windows-based applications, such as Microsoft Word for Windows (a word processor), Borland Quattro Pro for Windows (a spreadsheet), and Paradox for Windows (a database program), function in a similar manner to Windows. Therefore, once you master the following operations, you will have a very good idea of how to use other Windows-based software.

Will you make mistakes when working with Windows? In one word: yes. Everyone makes mistakes when working with software. The key is to remain relaxed, and when you make a mistake, look at your options on the screen. You'll find it is normally quite easy to exit an activity that was accidently started.

Two important keys for the beginning Windows user to remember are the Esc key and the F1 (first function) key. Pressing the Esc key allows you to escape or back out of many of the Windows screens. Pressing the F1 key accesses the on-line (on-screen) Help facility which explains most Windows commands and procedures.

When working in Windows, the view displayed on your monitor screen is referred to as the **desktop.** The desktop concept is used to simulate the setting people commonly use to write a report. During the writing process, people often surround themselves with stacks of material and then pull pieces of information from the various stacks. The **stacks** for a Windows user are the open applications and accessories displayed on the monitor screen (the desktop).

Most Windows users control the appearance of their desktop through the use of a mouse. The following section reviews the basic mouse commands. After completing that section, we'll begin our first Windows exercise.

Mouse Maneuvers

Usually, the mouse is installed (set up with the computer system) for a right-handed user. In these cases, the *left* mouse button is used to access most of the Windows commands. (To accommodate left-handed mouse users, the functions of the buttons may be changed through the mouse installation program or the Windows Control Panel.)

The six primary mouse actions are listed below.

Pointing: moving the mouse so that the tip of the pointer rests on the item of choice.

Clicking: pressing and releasing the mouse button once.

Double-clicking: rapidly pressing and releasing the mouse button twice, without moving the mouse.

Choosing: pointing and clicking (or double-clicking) on an item to initiate an action.

Selecting: pointing and clicking on a item to mark it (selecting does not in-itiate an action).

Dragging: pointing on an item, pressing the button, and holding it down while moving the mouse. This causes the pointer and the item to move across the screen to a new location. When the item is in the desired loca-tion, release the button to complete the procedure. (This feature is some-times referred to as "drag-and-drop.")

Starting Windows

Complete the following steps to start Windows on your computer.

1 Turn on your computer system and display the C:\> prompt on your screen. (Or, if Windows is loaded on a different drive, display that drive prompt and write the drive name on top of the letter "C" in the previous sentence).

2 As shown below, key the word **WIN** (in upper or lower case) at the DOS prompt and press Enter.
C:\>WIN (Press Enter.)

TIP: Usually, adding a WIN line to the end of your AUTOEXEC.BAT file will enable Windows to automatically load each time you **boot** (turn on) your computer.

Depending upon your hardware and how Windows is installed, the starting (also referred to as loading or launching) process usually takes 10–35 seconds. The Windows logo is displayed on the screen at the start of the process. The logo is then replaced with a blank screen, which is soon followed by a picture of a small hour glass. The hour glass icon is displayed on the screen whenever a Windows-based application is being loaded. The hour glass icon is then replaced by the first window of the program.

If your screen displays the phrase "Bad command or file name," you need to change to the directory holding Windows. Change to the proper directory and try the WIN command again. If Windows still does not load, refer to the "Troubleshooting" section of your Windows documentation.

The **Program Manager window** (the term "Program Manager" is listed in the window title bar; see Figure 1.1) is usually the first window to appear on your screen. The Program Manager window is sometimes referred to as a Windows shell program because it serves as a *Windows nerve center* from which you control many of your computing activities, such as starting and ending your Windows sessions and starting other computer programs. Because the goal of this chapter is to help you get started with Windows, only a few of the Program Manager features are explained here. Chapter Three is devoted entirely to the Program Manager application and provides the in-depth information needed to fully utilize the program.

NOTE: Windows is initially set up to display the Main window inside of the Program Manager window (as in Figure 1.1). If someone else has installed Windows for you, your initial screen may look somewhat different than Figure 1.1. As long as you see the Program Manager window, you will be able to complete the first few exercises in the chapter. When additional windows are to be displayed, you will be given the appropriate instructions for opening the needed windows.

Exiting and Restarting Windows

Toward the end of this chapter you will learn numerous ways to exit Windows. Just in case you need to leave the program before finishing the chapter, you may use the following steps to exit the program.

NOTE: The location of the **tip** of the on-screen pointer controls which area of the screen will be affected when the mouse button is pressed. When you are instructed to move the pointer to a particular location, try to place the tip of the pointer in the center of that area. The initial exercises emphasize moving the tip of the pointer to certain locations. Later in the chapter, after you gain some experience with the mouse, you will be instructed to just "point" to the appropriate location.

1   Using the mouse, move the tip of the pointer onto the word FILE (which is located on the left side of the menu bar, just below the Control-menu box and the Program Manager title bar), and click once.

This mouse action results in a list of commands being displayed under the word FILE. This list of commands is referred to as a **drop-down menu** (see Figure 1.2).

2   Move the tip of the pointer to the phrase Exit Windows... (the last choice on the FILE drop-down menu), and click once.

This mouse action causes the Exit Windows dialog box to appear on the desktop (see Figure 1.3). **Dialog boxes** are rectangular frames that appear on top of the window(s) you are working with to provide important information and to request a user response regarding the next computer activity.

Many dialog boxes ask you to confirm the previous command by moving the pointer tip on top of the **OK button** (the small shaded rectangle, inside the

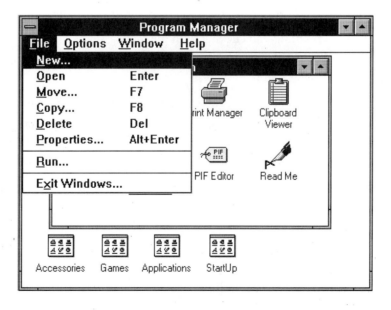

Figure 1.2   The Program Manager FILE drop-down menu.

Figure 1.3   The Exit Windows dialog box.

dialog box, containing the letters OK) and clicking once. To cancel the previous command, move the pointer on top of the **Cancel button** and click once.

3   To confirm that you want to exit Windows, choose the OK button (move the pointer on top of the OK button and click once).
        This action returns you to the screen you saw before you started Windows.

4   To restart Windows, follow the same directions that you previously used to load Windows. (The default setting—the one that Windows is initially programmed to use—is to type WIN at the C:\> prompt and press Enter).

5   Repeat steps 1–4 until you are comfortable starting and exiting the program.

As you learn to run Windows, you may prefer to exit Windows in other ways. However, the steps you just completed exposed you to some of the standard procedures used to operate Windows, including:

- pointing and clicking with the mouse,

- activating the menu bar and choosing commands from the drop-down menus, and

- confirming an action by clicking on the OK button in a dialog box.

In the following sections, we will use the Program Manager window and various mouse actions to practice additional basic Windows operations.

Minimizing, Maximizing, and Restoring Windows

Because Windows allows you to run many programs at once, you may often have a number of open windows on your desktop. Although there are ways to neatly arrange the open windows (more on this later), you'll probably find instances when you want to focus on only one or two windows. In these cases, you may choose to **minimize** some of the other open windows.

Minimizing a window reduces it to an icon that is displayed along the lower portion of the screen. The application is still available to you; its window is just out of the way. Each Windows application has its own distinctive icon (with the program name listed below it) to quickly remind you of its existence.
Either of the following steps minimizes a window:

1. Click once on the window's minimize button (the button, containing a down arrow, located to the right of the title bar; see Figure 1.1).

2. Click once on the Control-menu box (the box containing a dash, located in the upper-left corner of the window) to display the drop-down Control menu. Then choose (point on and click) the menu's Minimize command.

To return a minimized window to its previous size and location, you **restore** the window. Either of the following steps restores a minimized window:

1. Double-click on the corresponding icon located along the lower portion of the desktop.

NOTE: First-time "mousers" (mouse users) may have to practice double-clicking. If you accidently move the mouse during the first click you may see the icon move a little—just steady your hand on the work surface and try again. If you wait too long between clicks, the Control menu (the same menu that is displayed by clicking on the Control-menu box in an open window) may appear to "pop up" from the icon. To turn the menu off, move the pointer outside of the menu and click once. Then try double-clicking on the icon again.

2. Click once on the corresponding icon to display the Control menu. Choose (point on and click) the Restore command to redisplay the window.

Complete the exercise below to practice minimizing and restoring the Program Manager Window.

1 Minimize the Program Manager window by placing the tip of the pointer on top of the minimize button and clicking once. (The Program Manager window should now be reduced to an icon that appears similar to the icon shown in Figure 1.4.)

2 Restore the Program Manager window by double-clicking on its icon.

3 Minimize the Program Manager window again by clicking on the minimize button.

4 Restore the window by clicking once on the Program Manager icon to display the Control menu. Click on the Restore command to redisplay the window.

Figure 1.4   The Program Manager icon.

5 Repeat steps 1–4 until you are comfortable minimizing and restoring the Program Manager window.

If you want to see as much of the contents of a window as possible, **maximize** the window. Do this by clicking on the window's maximize button (the small button, containing an upward arrow, located in the top right corner of the window; see Figure 1.1).

Because Program Manager is a Windows application, the Program Manager window can contain other windows (such as the Main window). When an application window is maximized, the window fills the entire desktop and its double-line window borders are no longer visible (see Figure 1.5). When a window contained inside an application window is maximized, it fills the available work area within the current size of the application window.

NOTE: One of the most frightening things to happen to new users is to attempt to maximize a window and, instead, reduce it to an icon. In this case the minimize, instead of the maximize button, was chosen. If this happens to you, either restore the window to its previous size and then click on the maximize button, or click once on the minimized window icon to display the "pop up" Control menu and then choose the Maximize command.

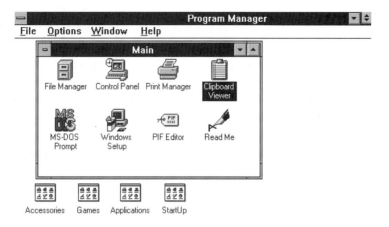

Figure 1.5 The maximized Program Manager window.

To restore a maximized Program Manager window to its previous size and location, you again click on the small box in the upper-right corner of the Program Manager window. Note that once a window is maximized, the maximize button is replaced with the **restore button** (see Figure 1.5). The restore button contains an up and down arrow. Clicking on this button causes the window to return to its previous size and position.

Complete the steps below to practice maximizing and restoring the Program Manager window.

1 Maximize the Program Manager window by placing the tip of the pointer on top of the maximize button and clicking once. (The Program Manager window should now fill your entire screen and look similar to Figure 1.5.)

2 Restore the Program Manager window to its original size by clicking once on the restore button.

3 Repeat the above steps until you are comfortable maximizing and restoring the window.

TIP: Another way to work with the maximize and restore functions is to double-click on the window's title bar, instead of clicking on the button in the upper-right corner of the window. To maximize a window, double-click on its title bar. To restore a maximized window, double-click on its title bar.

Sizing and Moving Windows

Sometimes it's more advantageous to change the size of a window, or move it, instead of minimizing or maximizing it. Window sizing and moving techniques are described below.

Although the windows always remain rectangular, you may change the *size* of most windows by completing the following steps:

1. Move the tip of the pointer onto the top, bottom, left, or right window border. This causes the pointer to change to a double-headed arrow.

2. Depress the mouse button and move the mouse to drag the selected border in or out of the existing window. While the original border stays in place, a second border (it looks like a thin zipper) is displayed to indicate the new window size being created. When the "zipper-like" border is in the desired location, release the mouse button to establish the new border and resize the window.

TIP: | To cancel the sizing procedure, press Esc before releasing the mouse button.

Moving the left or right border changes the horizontal window dimension. Moving the top or bottom border changes the vertical window dimension. To change both dimensions at once:

1. Move the pointer onto a corner of the window. This causes the pointer to become a diagonal double-headed arrow.

2. Drag the corner of the border to the desired location and release the mouse button.

TIP: | For many people, the most difficult sizing task is moving the tip of the pointer on top of the window border. You may have to work a little at this the first few times. Once you are near the border, slow your mouse movements until you see the pointer change to a double-headed arrow. Occasionally, although you are positioned correctly, the arrow still may not change to a double-headed arrow. Normally, when this happens one of the words in the menu bar has been selected (a selected menu bar choice appears in reverse video); press Esc, Alt, or click the mouse once (not on an icon, sizing button, or menu choice) to turn the menu off. Then repeat your sizing attempt.

Practice changing the size of the Program Manager window by completing the following steps:

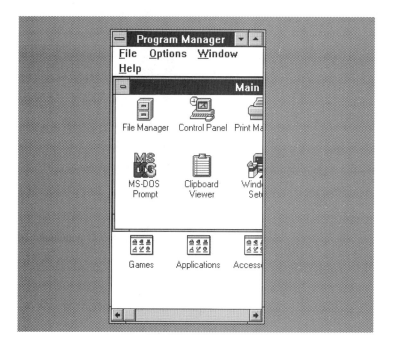

Figure 1.6 The Program Manager window after completing the sizing exercise.

1 If the Program Manager window is maximized or minimized, you do not have access to any of its borders. Display the window in its restored state, and then move each border approximately one inch inside the edge of the screen.

2 Shrink the size of the Program Manager window to approximately a three-inch square, in the middle of your screen, by dragging diagonally opposite corners toward the center. This action may cause "scroll bars" to appear on the lower and/or right side of the window. (Figure 1.6 displays a scroll bar along the bottom of the window.) **Scroll bars** indicate that the window holds more information than is currently visible. Working with scroll bars is addressed in the next section.

3 Change the height of the window to approximately six inches by expanding the top and bottom borders. (When you finish this step, your window may look similar to Figure 1.6.)

Throughout the rest of the text (and all of your work with Windows-based applications) you will continually be sizing windows to meet your needs.

To *move* a window, you simply drag it to a new location on the desktop by completing the following two steps:

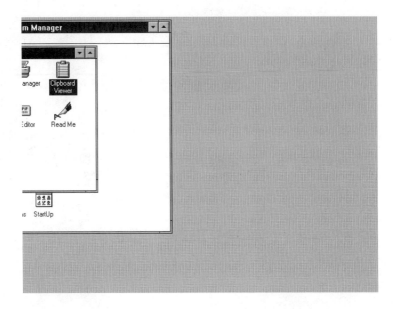

Figure 1.7 Half of the Program Manager window displayed on the desktop.

1. Place the pointer on top of the window's title bar.
2. Depress the mouse button and drag the window to its new position. Then, when the window is in the desired location, release the mouse button.

You may not move a maximized window because it already covers the entire desktop. Practice moving the Program Manager window by completing the steps below.

1 Size the Program Manager window to fill approximately half of the desktop (the screen area).

2 Move the Program Manager window to the top of the desktop by placing the tip of the pointer on the Program Manager title bar and dragging the window upward. Once the pointer reaches the top of the desktop, release the mouse button. Note that you may not move the pointer past the top of the desktop.

3 Place the pointer in the middle of the Program Manager title bar and drag the window as far left as possible. While half of the window may have been moved outside of the desktop (see Figure 1.7), you should not have been able to move the pointer outside of the desktop. (You have not lost half of the window; it merely is not displayed at this time.)

4   Return the entire window to the desktop by dragging the title bar to the right until the whole window is displayed.

5   Center the window on your desktop.

> NOTE: In the exercise above you saw that you could not move the pointer off the top or left side of the desktop. You may move most, but not all, of the pointer off the bottom or right side of the desktop.

The ability to move windows will also be very helpful as you learn to work with a number of open windows on your screen.

Scroll Bars

Scroll bars are indicators showing that the window holds more information than what you are currently seeing (see Figure 1.8).

A scroll bar consists of beginning and ending scroll arrows, the bar itself, and the scroll box. On a vertical scroll bar, the beginning scroll arrow points up, the ending arrow points down. On a horizontal scroll bar, the beginning arrow points left and the end arrow points right. The **scroll box** slides along the scroll bar to indicate the point in the window you are viewing. For example, in Figure 1.8 the scroll box is at the beginning of each scroll bar, which indicates the viewer is seeing the top-left portion of the contents in the Program Manager window.

Complete the steps below to display scroll bars on the Program Manager window.

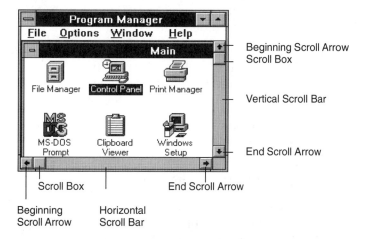

Figure 1.8 The Program Manager window with scroll bars.

1. Size the Program Manager window to fill most of the desktop by adjusting its borders accordingly.

2. If the Main window is not already open, look toward the bottom of the screen to locate the icon with the word "Main" listed below it. Upon finding the Main window icon, place the pointer on it and double-click. This action opens the Main window inside the Program Manager window.

   Minimize any other open windows inside the Program Manager window, then move the Main window into the upper left portion of the Program Manager window.

3. Drag the lower-right corner of the Program Manager window toward the upper-left corner of the desktop to form a four-inch-square Program Manager window. When you release the mouse button, you will have added scroll bars to the Program Manager window (see Figure 1.8).

   If you do not want to change the size of the window to display its contents, you need to scroll through the window's work area. Use any of the following methods to scroll through the work area of a window:

   1. Click on the scroll bar's beginning or ending scroll arrow. This action moves the window contents one line at a time. (The direction of movement depends upon which arrow is clicked.) If the mouse button is held down, the contents continuously scroll by.

   2. Click on either side of the scroll box (on the scroll bar), to move the contents through part of the window work area.

   3. Drag the scroll box along the scroll bar with the mouse. This is the fastest way to jump to a new location. (However, the contents do not scroll through the window as you drag the box.) This action is especially useful when working with long, ordered, lists.

   The exercise below demonstrates how to use the scroll bars. Remember that as the appearance of the contents in the window changes, the actual contents do not change; you are just viewing a different portion of the information. Complete the following steps using the vertical scroll bar.

1. Move the tip of the pointer onto the end scroll arrow (down arrow) and watch the window as you click the mouse button once. The contents inside the screen move, as does the vertical scroll box.

2. Repeat step 1 and watch the movements again.

3. Move the pointer to the beginning scroll arrow (up arrow) and click once. The contents of the window should move down in the window and the scroll box should move higher. Repeat this step again.

4   Move the pointer to the end scroll arrow (down arrow), press the mouse button, and keep the button depressed while the contents of the window scroll toward the top of the window. The scroll box is now at the bottom of the bar.

5   Reverse step 4 by placing the pointer on the beginning arrow scroll, pressing the mouse button, and keeping it depressed while the contents of the window scroll toward the bottom.

6   Drag the scroll box to various locations on the bar and observe the changes in the window contents when you release the mouse button.

7   Move the scroll box to the center of the bar and click (on the scroll bar) above the box. Again, you should notice changes in the window contents.

For further practice, resize the Program Manager window and repeat the steps on either of the scroll bars.

TIP: Upon seeing a scroll bar on a window, many people choose to enlarge the window to see as much information as possible. If a scroll bar still appears after enlarging a window, click on the beginning scroll arrow, or drag the scroll box back to the beginning of the scroll bar. Either of these actions removes the scroll bar if the newly sized window is large enough to display the entire window contents. If a scroll bar remains on the screen, the window still is not large enough to display all of its contents.

Application and Document Windows

The two basic types of windows you will work with are **application windows** and **document windows.**

You control the applications that come with Windows (such as Program Manager) and Windows-based applications (like the WordPerfect for Windows word processing package and the Microsoft Excel spreadsheet program) through their application windows. Opening an application window activates its corresponding program. (For the purposes of this text, the terms application and program are used interchangeably.) Most application windows are similar in appearance, and they all display a menu bar below the window title bar.

A document window is located *inside* an application window. Document windows usually contain the data files you are working with. They do not have a menu bar—they share the application's menu. Some applications have no document windows, whereas other applications may contain several overlapping document windows.

Up to this point you have worked primarily with an application window—the Program Manager window. The next exercise utilizes the Main window (which is a document window) to demonstrate that, for the most part, document windows operate in the same way as application windows.

1 Expand the Program Manager window to fill most of the desktop by dragging its window borders toward the edges of the screen.

2 If the Main window is open, reduce it to an icon by clicking on its minimize button. (Reduce any other document windows inside the Program Manager window to icons.)

3 Restore the Main window by double-clicking on its icon.

4 Maximize the Main window by clicking on its maximize button.

NOTE: When a document window is maximized, it covers all the work area of the application window. The title bar of a maximized document window is removed, and the name of the document window appears in the title bar of the application window (see Figure 1.9). The restore button for the document window appears below the sizing button in the upper-right corner of the application window. A maximized document window does not necessarily cover the entire desktop.

5 Restore the Main window to its previous size and location by clicking on its restore button.

6 Size the Main window (adjust the window borders) to remove any scroll bars from it, but do not let the Main window cover all of the work space in the Program Manager window.

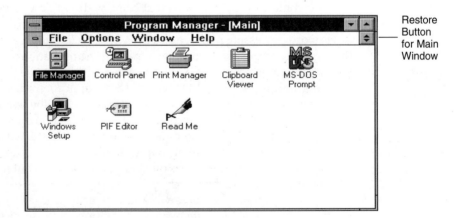

Figure 1.9 The Program Manager window containing a maximized Main window.

| 7 | Move the Main window, by dragging its title bar, to a number of different screen locations.

NOTE: As you completed step 7, you undoubtedly noticed that you could not display any part of the Main window *outside* the Program Manager. Document windows can be displayed only inside their application window.

Group Windows

As previously stated, the Program Manager window is designed to serve as the starting point for your Windows operations. The Program Manager document windows are different from other document windows because, instead of containing typical text, numbers, or graphic images, they hold the means for starting the various programs that can be launched from the Program Manager. Similar types of programs may be clustered together in the same window. Because of this grouping concept, the document windows in Program Manager are referred to as *group* windows.

When Windows is first installed, Program Manager has at least four group windows—Main, Accessories, Games, and Startup. Another group, "Applications," may be created during the initial set up. Programs found in the Applications group may include Windows-based programs and non-Windows (or DOS-based) programs (i.e., DOS versions of WordPerfect and Lotus 1-2-3).

A group window may be minimized to a group icon, which is usually located along the bottom of the Program Manager work area. Group icons look like miniature windows with a title bar and two rows of symbols. The corresponding group names are placed below each symbol.

So far, we've been working with the Program Manager and Main windows. It's time to open a few more windows on our desktop.

| 1 | In the previous exercise you worked with the Main window inside the Program Manager window. Move and size the Program Manager and Main windows to display the remaining group window icons in the Program Manager window.

| 2 | Open the Accessories group window by double clicking on the Accessories icon. The Accessories window appears inside the Program Manager window and may cover a portion of the Main window. (Do not be alarmed if this happens; you already know how to move and size windows.)

| 3 | If the Games icon is not visible, move or size the Main or Accessories window to expose the icon. When you can see any part of the Games icon, double-click on it to open the Games group window.

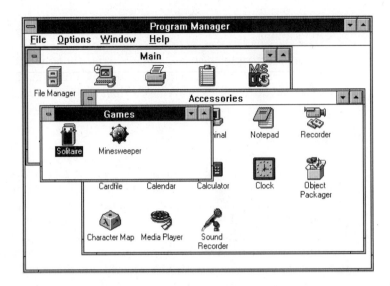

Figure 1.10   The Games, Main, and Accessories windows displayed within the Program Manager window.

After you complete this step, your screen may be similar to the one in Figure 1.10. Because the Games window was the last window opened, it appears on top of the other windows and its title bar is highlighted.

4   Resize and move the Main, Accessories, and Games windows to three different areas of the Program Manager window. (This is a good time to use the Maximize button on the Program Manager window.) Try to make sure that part of the title bar shows on each of the three windows.

Active and Inactive Windows

Arranging all three windows as instructed above may have provided some good practice with sizing and moving techniques and use of the mouse. Did you notice that as you clicked on a window, that window became the top window (often covering parts of the other windows) and its title bar became brighter than the other group window title bars?

The window with the highlighted title bar is the **active,** or **current window.** Depending upon their arrangement, the active window may overlap other windows. Only one document window can be current, or active, at one time. The remaining document windows are considered to be **inactive.**

A window may be moved or sized only if it is the active window. To make a window active, click on it.

TIP: While you can click on any area of an inactive window to make it active, you may want to avoid clicking on the Control-menu box or the sizing buttons. Clicking on an inactive window's Control-menu box makes the window active and displays its Control menu. (You would probably need to close the menu before proceeding with your desired action.) Clicking on an inactive window's minimize button reduces the window to an icon. Clicking on an inactive window's maximize button makes the window active and maximizes it.

The following exercise provides additional practice in changing the open window. Note the change in the title bar when a window becomes active.

1 Place the pointer on the work area of the Main window and click once to make the Main window active.

2 Make the Games window active by clicking on it.

3 Make the Accessories window active by clicking on it.

4 Minimize all the group windows, leaving only the Program Manager window open.

At this point, you have already learned to control your Windows environment through the use of the mouse and various Windows elements (i.e., icons, sizing buttons, and window borders). In the next section, you will learn how to access numerous program commands through the use of drop-down menus.

Working with Menus

A menu may be defined as a list of related commands that may be used with the current application. Most Windows applications have numerous menus. The names of the menus are listed in the application's menu bar (located directly below its title bar). The Program Manager menu bar includes the FILE, OPTIONS, WINDOW, and HELP menus (see Figure 1.11).

To display the commands listed under a word on the menu bar, move the tip of the pointer onto the desired word and click once. (Using the keyboard to access the menu is discussed later in this chapter.) This action will display a list of commands underneath the word that was chosen. These lists are called **drop-down menus** because the choices appear to "drop down" from the top

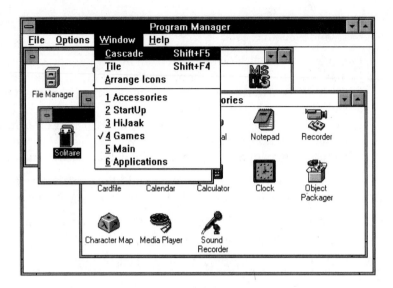

Figure 1.11 The Program Manager WINDOW drop-down menu.

word. Figure 1.11 displays the choices in Program Manager's drop-down WINDOW menu.

Drop-down menus are a key element in the Windows graphical environment because they enable the user to view and choose numerous commands without having to leave the current screen. While most menu commands may be accessed at any point, a command appearing in dimmed letters indicates it may not be activated at the current time and position in the program.

An ellipsis following a drop-down menu command indicates that when that command is chosen, a dialog box will appear. You have already used this type of command when you completed the "Exiting and Restarting Windows" section earlier in this chapter. You opened the FILE menu and chose the "Exit Windows..." command which displayed the "Exit Windows" dialog box. (Dialog boxes are covered in the next chapter.)

NOTE: An example of how menu commands will be listed in the text is shown below.

FILE-Exit Windows...

In this example, the capitalized word corresponds to the same word on the menu bar (FILE corresponds to the word "File" on the menu bar). The word, or phrase, following the dash after the menu bar choice, is the identified command from the drop-down menu (Exit Windows... corresponds to the "Exit Windows..." command on the drop-down menu).

In the following sections you'll learn more about menus and how they can control the appearance of your desktop.

The WINDOW Menu

There will be times when you need to keep a number of open windows on your desktop. If you have many windows open at once, continually moving and sizing individual windows may become quite tedious, and you may accidently totally cover an open window. The Cascade and Tile commands, on the WINDOW menu, enable you to instantly arrange and identify all of the windows inside the application window.

The **WINDOW-Cascade** command is designed to show all of the open document windows in a downward step display. Each window is the same size and the last window opened (the active window) is fully exposed in the foreground of the desktop. Usually, the active window is positioned as the bottom step of the cascade. The title bars from the previously opened windows are displayed (in the order in which they were opened) in the background. In the example shown in Figure 1.12, the Main window was opened first, followed by the Accessories window, while the Games window was the last to be opened.

In Figure 1.12, the easiest way to make the Main or Accessories window active would be to click on the desired window's title bar. Making another

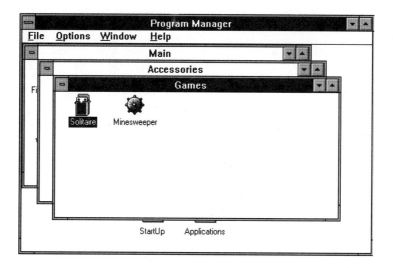

Figure 1.12 Cascaded Main, Accessories, and Games windows.

window active would change the desktop appearance. You would need to choose the WINDOW-Cascade command again to redisplay the windows in a cascaded format, with the new active window displayed in the foreground.

There will be times when you need to work in two or more windows at the same time. The **WINDOW-Tile** command resizes and arranges the open windows inside the application window, to allow the user to view all of the open document windows simultaneously (see Figure 1.13). When the WINDOW-Tile command is used, it is common to see scroll bars on the document windows.

The exercise below provides practice for cascading and tiling the group windows inside the Program Manager window.

1 (The Program Manager window should already be open and filling all (or most) of the desktop. All document windows should be minimized.) Open the Main, Accessories, and Games windows.

2 Choose (point and click on) the WINDOW option from the Program Manager menu bar. Your screen should resemble Figure 1.11. If another menu is showing, move the pointer to the word WINDOW and click.

3 Choose the WINDOW-Cascade command (click on the word Cascade listed in the WINDOW menu) to view the three windows arranged on your screen in a manner similar to the windows in Figure 1.12.

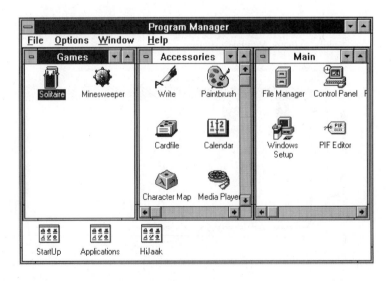

Figure 1.13 Tiled Games, Accessories, and Main windows.

4 | Choose the WINDOW-Tile command to view the three windows placed in vertical thirds of the Program Manager window. Your screen should look similar to the one shown in Figure 1.13.

The Program Manager WINDOW menu also includes the **Arrange Icons** command. If a group window is active when this command is chosen, the icons in the group window will be placed into rows. If a group icon is selected when this command is chosen, all group icons will be arranged in rows.

TIP: | The lower section of the WINDOW menu lists all the minimized or open windows in the application's work area. In Figure 1.11, there are six open or minimized windows that can be accessed. The checkmark next to Games indicates it is the active window. Clicking on the name of another window will make that window active. Clicking on the name of a minimized window will restore it to its previous size and location.

Accessing Menus with the Keyboard

Some Windows users choose to use the keyboard to utilize menus. Follow the steps below to access a menu from the keyboard.

1. Press Alt to activate the menu bar. Once the menu is active, the first word on the far left (normally "FILE") is selected—the background around the word changes and the lettering appears in reverse print.

2. To open a drop-down menu, press the key corresponding to the underlined letter of your menu choice (i.e., F for FILE, W for WINDOW, etc.).

3. To choose a command from the drop-down menu, press the underlined character shown in the desired command. Or you may use the cursor control keys to move up or down the list to your choice and then press the Enter key. Tapping a non-underlined character results in the computer beeping to indicate that Windows does not know what action to take. If this happens to you, just choose a character again.

4. Closing a menu automatically occurs when you choose a command. To leave the menu bar without choosing a command, press Alt; or press Esc until no word on the menu bar is selected.

Shortcut Keys

Some drop-down menu commands have **shortcut keys** assigned to them. These are single or combination keystrokes that enable you to execute a command without using the menu bar. (The shortcut key commands do not work when the menu is activated.) Complete the following exercise to practice using the shortcut keys.

1 With the Main, Accessories, and Games windows open inside the Program Manager window, open the drop-down WINDOW menu by clicking on the word WINDOW in the menu bar.

2 Note that key combination Shift+F5 appears after the Cascade command. This indicates that, when the menu is closed, holding down the Shift key and pressing the fifth function key arranges the document windows into a cascade format.

3 Press Esc to close the drop-down menu. Press Esc to leave the menu bar.

4 Press Shift+F5 to arrange your windows in a cascade format.

5 Open the WINDOW menu by pressing Alt, and pressing W to view the shortcut keys for tiling the application window, then close the menu.

6 Use the appropriate shortcut keys to tile the windows inside the Program Manager window. (Hint: Press Shift+F4.)

As you use Windows, you will probably find that you are utilizing both the mouse and the keyboard (especially when using menus). Using the keyboard provides access to the numerous shortcut key combinations. However, don't try to memorize all of the combinations because some shortcuts will be used more often than others. You will likely memorize commonly used key combinations without even trying.

Closing Windows and Exiting Programs

To protect the time and effort you invested to create a document, *always* be sure to properly exit your computer program(s) before turning off the computer. In Windows, the typical exiting procedure includes:

- saving new and revised files;
- closing the open document windows;
- closing the applications that were used; and
- closing the Program Manager window.

Saving files is discussed in later chapters. Since there are no files to save at this point, we will move to closing document windows.

Closing Document Windows

Closing a document window may be accomplished through the use of its Control-menu box (the small box, containing a dash, located in the upper-left corner of the window). Clicking once on this box activates the Control menu, which gives the user options to size, move, or close a window. The Control menu commands are listed below.

Command	Action
Restore	Returns a window to its previous size and location.
Move	Allows you to move a window using the cursor control keys.
Size	Allows you to change the size of a window using the cursor control keys.
Minimize	Decreases the window to an icon.
Maximize	Enlarges the window to fill the application's work area.
Close	Closes the window.
Next	Activates the next open document or group window within the application window. (The "next" window is based upon the order in which the windows were originally opened.)

For applications windows . . .

Switch To	Allows you to choose another running application.

Two ways to close a window using the control-menu box are:

1. Click once on the Control-menu box to activate its drop-down menu, then choose the Close command; or,

2. Double-click on the Control-menu box.

A document window may also be closed without the use of the Control-menu box. Pressing the shortcut key combination corresponding to the Close command on the Control menu (CTRL+F4) closes a document window. The shortcut key combination for closing an application window is ALT+F4.

In the exercise below you will close the Main, Accessories, and Games group windows that were used in the previous exercise. (If these windows are not open on your desktop, open them before starting the following exercise.)

1 Close the Games window by clicking once on its Control-menu box and then choosing the Close command from the drop-down menu.

2 Close the Accessories window by double-clicking on its Control-menu box.

3 The Main window should now be active. (It's the only document window still open.) Close this window by using the appropriate shortcut key combination. (Hint: Press Ctrl+F4.)

Closing the Program Manager and Exiting Windows

Normally, you will be running at least one application in addition to Program Manager. If you are working on a document in another Windows-based application, and you try to exit Windows by closing the Program Manager window, Windows displays a dialog box asking if you want to save the open document before exiting Windows. If you have a non-Windows application open, you need to close the application before exiting Windows.

Application windows can be closed by any of the following methods:

1. Double-clicking on the Control-menu box.

2. Single clicking on the Control-menu box to display the drop-down menu, and then choosing the Close command.

3. Clicking on the FILE menu choice to display the drop-down menu, then choosing the Exit command.

4. Pressing the shortcut key combination of Alt+F4.

Follow any of these approaches to close Program Manager. All four methods activate the Windows safety net—which is an "Exit Windows" dialog box that includes a message stating you are about to end your Windows session. This safety net is designed to prevent you from accidently exiting Windows before you are ready. You are instructed to choose one of the two options presented in the Exit Windows dialog box. If you are not ready to exit Windows, click on Cancel; if you are, click on OK. (You may also remove the dialog box by pressing Esc.)

To practice ending your Windows sessions and using a dialog box, complete the following:

1 Click on the Control-menu box, in the Program Manager window, to display the Control menu. Click on Close. Click on the Cancel button in the Exit Windows dialog box. (This action voids the exiting procedure and returns you to the Program Manager window.)

2 Use the shortcut key combination of Alt+F4 to reach the Exit Windows dialog box. Click on the Cancel button in the dialog box.

3 Double-click on the Control-box menu. Click on the Cancel button in the dialog box.

4 Click on the word FILE in the menu bar and then choose the Exit Windows... command. Click on the OK button to exit Windows.

Summary

Windows works with DOS to provide a **graphical user interface (GUI)** between the user and the computer. The Windows environment replaces the standard DOS prompt (i.e., C:\>) with screen windows, icons, menus, and dialog boxes. The GUI allows for most DOS operations to be accomplished without issuing a single character-based DOS command.

The **primary parts of a window** are: borders, Control-menu box, title bar, minimize and maximize (and restore) buttons, work area, icons, and, for Windows-based applications, a menu bar.

Drop-down menus provide a list of commands that can be activated through using the mouse or the keyboard. Each choice on the menu bar has a corresponding drop-down menu.

The **primary mouse activities** are: pointing, clicking, double-clicking, dragging, choosing, and selecting.

To **enlarge a window** to cover the desktop, or the application window's work area, click on the maximize button. To return the window to its previous size and location, click on the restore button.

To **reduce the window to an icon,** click on the minimize button. Double-click on a minimized window icon to restore the window to its previous size and location.

Adjust the size of a window by moving its borders inside or outside of their current position.

Move the window by dragging its title bar to the desired location.

Scroll bars on windows indicate that the current size of the window is not large enough to display all of its contents; therefore, you must scroll through the information. Manipulate scroll bars by clicking on the beginning and ending scroll arrows, clicking on either side of the scroll box, or moving the **scroll box** along the scroll bar.

The correct **procedure for exiting Windows** includes: saving new and revised files, closing the document windows inside an application, closing the application(s), and (in most Windows installations) closing the Program Manager to end the Windows session.

━━━━━━━━━━━━━ **Applications** ━━━━━━━━━━━━━

Application 1

1. Load Windows.

2. Sketch the Program Manager window on a sheet of paper. Identify the key elements of the window; border, title bar, etc. Write a one- or two-sentence description of the role of each part of the window.

3. Exit Windows.

NOTE: The remaining applications require Windows to be loaded before starting. You may choose to start and exit Windows for each application. Or at the end of an application, you may close all windows except the Program Manager window.

Application 2

1. Open the Main and Accessories windows.

2. Reduce the Main and Accessories windows to four-inch squares and place one window on each side of the Program Manager window.

3. Use the scroll bars on each document window to view its contents.

4. Move the Accessories window to the top-right corner of the Program Manager work area. Move the Main window to the lower-left corner.

5. Shrink the Program Manager window to a five-inch square. Note what happens to the document windows.

6. Use the Program Manager scroll bars to view the window's contents.

7. Minimize the Program Manager window. Note what happens to the document windows.

8. Restore the Program Manager window to its five-inch square.

9. Using only one dragging action, resize the Program Manager window to a six-inch square.

10. Resize the Program Manager window to a three-inch by five-inch rectangle.

11. Maximize the Program Manager window.

12. Minimize the Main window.

13. Close the Accessories window.

Application 3

1. Open the Main, Accessories, and Games windows.

2. Use the mouse and appropriate menu to tile the windows in the Program Manager window.

3. Open the Startup window.

4. Use the ALT key and the corresponding letter to access the menu to allow you to tile the windows again.

5. Use the shortcut key combination to cascade the windows. (Remember, you cannot use the shortcut keys when a drop-down menu is displayed.)

6. Make the Main window the active window and note where it appears in relation to the other windows.

7. Close two of the document windows by double-clicking on the Control-menu box. Close one document window by choosing the Control menu-Close command. Close the last document window by using the keyboard shortcut method.

8. Exit Windows.

Application 4

1. On the same sheet of paper used for Application 1, record what you feel were the three most important concepts discussed in this chapter.

2. List the Chapter 1 concepts on which you would like to receive more information.

3. Be prepared to share your responses to Applications 1 and 4.

2

Working with Multiple Applications, Dialog Boxes, and Windows Help

We will complete our look at basic Windows operations in this chapter. The first exercises focus on keeping organized when you have a number of open Windows applications on your desktop.

Working with dialog boxes, a crucial component of the Windows environment, is covered next. When certain Windows commands are initiated, dialog boxes appear on the desktop to provide additional information and to request a user response. To learn the general methods for working with dialog boxes, you will work with the Desktop dialog box (which enables you to change the appearance of your Windows desktop).

Having the ability to instantly request help on almost any Windows topic can be quite reassuring for new Windows users. The chapter concludes by explaining how to use the on-line Windows Help facility.

Running Multiple Applications

Today's office worker may often use three software packages to create one document. Business reports typically consist of text (created with a word processor), columns of numbers (created with a spreadsheet package), and illustrations (created with a graphics program). Common problems associated with creating this type of report include:

1. The need to learn three different sets of commands to run the software programs.

2. Creating three separate files to hold the corresponding parts of the report.

3. Being able to run only one program at a time.

4. Merging the appropriate data from the three files into one document.

In the past, the merging process (item 4 above) was commonly done by printing the files from each program, physically cutting out the necessary parts from each printout, and pasting these pieces together on another sheet. (Later in the text, you will learn to use the Windows version of this "cut-and-paste" procedure.)

A person faced with this type of situation may benefit greatly by using Windows and Windows-based applications. Part of the power of Windows includes: having the ability to simultaneously run numerous applications on the desktop; using common commands in different applications; and being able to easily transfer information from various programs into one document.

You may simultaneously run multiple programs on your desktop because Windows automatically allows open programs to share the computer's memory and processing power. (Additional memory and a fast 80386 or 80486 central processing unit would greatly enhance your ability to concurrently run multiple programs. For more information on how Windows distributes the computer's resources to open applications, refer to your Windows documentation.)

Most of the applications that are designed to run in the Windows environment share a similar "look-and-feel." The similar *look* is provided by the applications' common on-screen appearance (including windows, icons, title bars, and menus). The similar *feel* is created by the programs utilizing the same procedures for completing standard tasks. For example, most Windows-based applications require similar steps for naming, saving, opening, closing, and printing files, and for transferring data from one application to another.

Numerous application windows can be displayed on the desktop, while their corresponding applications are completing program tasks, but only one application *window* may be **active** at one time. The remaining open applications are referred to as being **inactive.** Just as with document windows, the title bar of the active application window is displayed in a different shade than that of the title bars of the other windows. Also, the active application window will often cover parts of other windows.

NOTE: One additional concept concerning concurrently running applications is how the applications use the computer's memory and processing power. The active application is considered to be running in the **foreground** (which normally means it is using the majority of the computer's resources). The other applications are running in the **background,** and share the remaining computer resources. Because Windows allows for the computer's memory and processing power to be distributed among open applications, tasks from different programs may appear to be performed at the same time (i.e., searching for records in a database, while spell-checking a word processing document). Because the background programs do not have access to all the computer's resources, don't be surprised if procedures being run in the background programs take a little longer than usual to be executed.

In the following exercise you will use the Program Manager window as a shell, or starting point, from which to launch other Windows programs. The basic method for starting a program from the Program Manager window is to display the appropriate program group window and then double-click on the desired icon.

1 Start Windows by keying WIN at the C:\> prompt and displaying the Program Manager window.

2 Drag each border of the Program Manager window within approximately one inch of the corresponding outer edge of the desktop. (If your Program Manager window is maximized when it first appears, choose the restore button to display the borders of the window.)

3 If the Main window is not automatically displayed, place the tip of the pointer on the Main group icon (located near the bottom of the Program Manager window) and double-click on it to display the Main window.

4 Open the accessories window (if it is not already displayed).

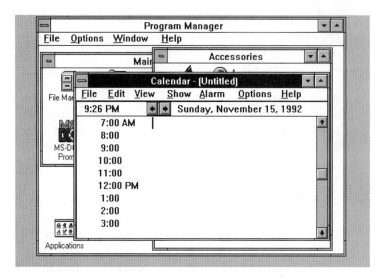

Figure 2.1   The Program Manager, Main, Accessories, and Calendar windows.

5   Place the pointer in the Main window (not on an icon, box or button) and click once to make the Main window active. Then try to move the Main window outside the Program Manager window by placing the pointer on the Main window's title bar and dragging it through the upper Program Manager window border. (You should not be able to do this.)

6   Make the Accessories window active and place it in the right half of the Program Manager window. If the Accessories window displays scroll bars, remove them by resizing the window. (Cover as much of the Main window as needed to fully display the Accessories window.)

7   Move the pointer inside the Accessories window. Point and double-click on the Calendar icon. (It looks like a typical daily desk calendar.) This action should result in the Calendar window appearing on your screen. Depending upon the size of your Calendar window, your desktop may resemble the one shown in Figure 2.1.

NOTE: If your Program Manager window was reduced to an icon when the Calendar window was displayed, the Program Manager OPTIONS-Minimize on Use command was most likely selected. This command reduces the Program Manager window to an icon whenever another application window is opened. If your Program Manager window has been reduced to an icon, double-click on the icon to open the Program Manager window. Then choose the OPTIONS command from the Program Manager menu bar. If a checkmark appears next to the Minimize on Use command, the command is already activated. Turn off the Minimize on Use command by choosing it again. Then complete the rest of this exercise.

One way to tell that the Calendar window is an application window, and not just a document window inside Program Manager, is to note the Calendar menu bar. Another way is to move the Calendar window outside the Program Manager window. Remember, document windows do not have menu bars, and they must stay inside their application window. Application windows can appear wherever you place them on the desktop.

8   Place the pointer on the Calendar window title bar and move this window outside the Program Manager window by dragging the title bar to the top-right corner of the desktop. (You should be able to do this.)
Size this window to cover the right third of the desktop.

To make matters more interesting, let's open a few programs from the Accessories group window. Later in the text, these accessories are explained in more detail. We use them now just to demonstrate running multiple applications simultaneously.

9   Point on the Cardfile icon, inside the Accessories window, and double-click on it to open the Cardfile accessory. (If the Cardfile icon is covered by the Calendar window, click on the Accessories window to make it active—this displays all the accessories.)

10   Size and move the Cardfile window to fill the lower-right quarter of the desktop. Make sure the Clock icon is visible in the Accessories window.

11   Point on the Clock icon, inside the Accessories window, and double-click on it to open the Clock accessory. Size and move the Clock window to fill the lower-left quarter of the desktop. (Note that the Clock program does not have a FILE menu choice.)

12   Point on the Write icon, inside the Accessories window, and double-click on it to open the Write accessory. When the Write window opens, locate the blinking vertical line (insertion point) in the upper-left part of the Write window work area and type your first and last name inside the window. (Use the left and right cursor keys and the backspace key for editing purposes.)
Then move the Write window to the upper-left portion of your desktop (overlap the Clock title bar with the Write window). Your window may look similar to Figure 2.2.

Leave the open windows on your desktop and complete the next section.

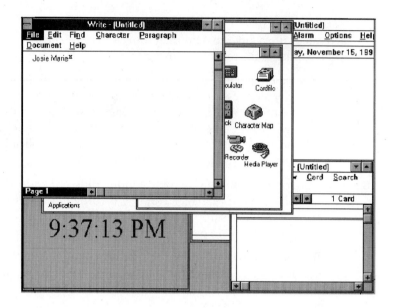

Figure 2.2 Results of the current exercise.

Cycling Through Open Applications

By now, your desktop may look quite cluttered. When many windows are opened on the desktop, some windows may become completely covered. When this happens, even experienced Windows users can become confused regarding which applications are currently in use. You know you can switch among applications by clicking on the desired window. However, if you can't see a window, you can't click on it.

One method for finding the desired window is to reduce other windows to icons until you find the one you want. There are easier ways.

You may cycle through the open programs on your desktop by holding down the Alt key and tapping the Esc key (this key combination is shown as Alt+Esc). Each time you press Alt+Esc, a different open application window or application icon is highlighted. (A highlighted window displays a shaded,

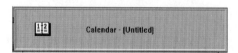

Figure 2.3 The program indicator box.

or brighter, title bar. This makes it easy to locate on a crowded desktop. When an application icon is highlighted, the icon moves to the desktop front and the program name, located below the symbol, is displayed in reverse video.) Pressing Alt+Esc will (eventually) bring a covered window to the front of the desktop. When the desired window, or icon, is highlighted, release the Alt key.

Another way to learn which applications are open is to hold down the Alt key and tap the Tab key. Each time you press Alt+Tab, a small title box appears in the center of the screen showing the name of an open application (see Figure 2.3). When you see the name of the desired program, release the Alt key to make that program active.

TIP: The Alt+Tab key combination lets you cycle through the open applications more quickly than the Alt+Esc key combination. The box displayed by pressing Alt+Tab is faster for Windows to display than re-drawing each application window. Also, many users prefer using the Alt+Tab combination because it is easier to stay focused on the center of the desktop than to scan the entire screen.

Practice cycling through your open applications by completing the following exercise. (This exercise builds on the previous exercise.)

1 Depress the Alt key (and keep it depressed) while tapping the Esc key to cycle through your open windows. Note that when the Program Manager window becomes current, you may also see the Accessories document window become active.

2 Use the Alt+Esc key combination to make the Clock window active.

3 Depress the Alt key (and keep it depressed) while tapping the Tab key to cycle through the boxes displaying the names of the open applications.

4 Use the Alt+Tab key combination to make the Program Manager window active.

In the previous chapter, the Program Manager WINDOW-Tile and WINDOW-Cascade commands were used to arrange the windows on the desktop. Try these commands again; you may be surprised at your results.

1 Choose the WINDOW-Tile command.

2 Choose the WINDOW-Cascade command.

All the open windows were not neatly rearranged. Why? Because the Program Manager WINDOW commands act on the document windows inside the Program Manager window. Most of the windows we opened were application windows, not Program Manager document windows; therefore, the Program Manager WINDOW commands had no effect on them.

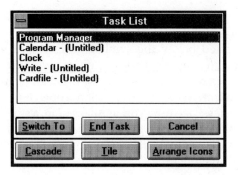

Figure 2.4 The Task List dialog box displaying the names of the applications opened in the previous exercises.

The Task List Utility

Another way to control your open applications is to use the Task List utility. The Task List is activated by either:

1. Pressing Ctrl+Esc, or

2. Pointing to any desktop space not occupied by a window and double-clicking.

When this utility is activated, the Task List dialog box appears on the desktop (see Figure 2.4). The top of this dialog box contains a rectangular frame displaying a list of the current open programs. (This frame is referred to as a **list box.**) The bottom part of the dialog box contains six buttons that, when chosen, enable the user to switch, close, and arrange the applications on the desktop.

NOTE: When working with the Task List utility, you will be *selecting* program names and *choosing* buttons. Selecting a program name consists of placing the tip of the pointer on the desired name and clicking the mouse button. (A selected program name appears in reverse video.) Choosing a button consists of pointing on the button and clicking the mouse button. (A button appears as a three-dimensional box within a window or dialog box. In some instructions in this text, the term "click on the _____ button" will be used in place of "choose the _____ button" to enhance the clarity of the given instruction.)

The functions of the Task List buttons follow.

Button	Function
Switch To	After selecting an application from the list box, choosing the Switch To button makes the selected application active. (Or you can make a program active by double-clicking on its name in the list box.)
End Task	Choosing the End Task button closes the selected application.
Cancel	Choosing the Cancel button closes Task List without taking any action. (Task List may also be closed by pressing Esc or by clicking on any window or icon. Task List automatically closes whenever a command is chosen.)
Cascade	Choosing the Cascade button arranges the open application windows into a "stair-step" pattern on your desktop.
Tile	Choosing the Tile button resizes and arranges the open application windows, on the desktop, to allow the user to view all of the open application windows at the same time.
Arrange Icons	Choosing the Arrange Icons button organizes the minimized application icons along the bottom of the desktop.

Practice using Task List by completing the following steps. (This exercise utilizes the open applications from the previous exercises.)

1 Activate Task List by using either method described above.

2 Choose the Tile button to rearrange your desktop. (Your desktop may now resemble the one shown in Figure 2.5.)

Begin each of the remaining steps by displaying the Task List dialog box on your desktop.

3 Select the Calendar program (from the list bar inside of Task List), and choose the Switch To button to make the Calendar window active. Then minimize the Calendar window and note its distinctive icon along the bottom of the desktop.

4 Activate the Write program (from Task List) by double-clicking on its name. Move and resize the window to completely cover the Clock window.

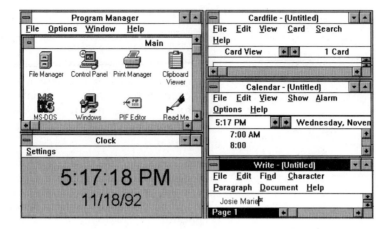

Figure 2.5 Typical results of choosing the Tile button in Task List.

5 | Make the Clock window active by double-clicking on its name (in Task List). Resize the window to a three-inch square and place it in the lower-right corner of the desktop.

6 | Open the Calendar window (from Task List) by double-clicking on its name.

7 | Close the Clock application by selecting it from the list box inside of Task List and then choosing the End Task button.

8 | Choose the Cascade button to rearrange your desktop. (Your desktop may look similar to Figure 2.6.)

9 | Minimize each of the remaining windows, then scatter the icons on the desktop. Open Task List and choose the Arrange Icons button to rearrange your icons.

10 | Open the Program Manager window (from Task List) by selecting it from the list of programs and choosing the Switch To button.

NOTE: A Windows application will display a "safety net" dialog box if the latest revisions of an open file have not been saved and the user attempts to exit the program. The dialog box indicates that, if the program is closed at this point, the latest version of the document will not be saved.

11 | Select the name of the Write program and choose the End Task button. A dialog box appears warning you that you have not saved the changes on the current Write file (you entered your name when you first opened Write). Choose "No" to close the Write "safety net" dialog box and to close the application.

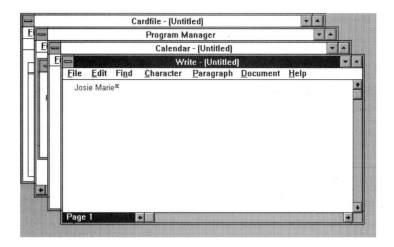

Figure 2.6 Cascaded desktop.

12 Use Task List to close all programs except the Program Manager.

As you worked with Task List, you probably noticed the first letter of each button (except the Cancel button) was underlined. You may execute any Task List button command, from the keyboard, by holding down the Alt key, and pressing the underlined letter. Pressing the Esc key will close Task List and remove the utility from the desktop.

The Task List Control-menu box (in the upper-left corner of the dialog box) contains two choices—Move or Close. The Close command closes the utility and removes it from the desktop. The Move command allows keyboard users to move the Task List box. The steps involved in moving the box, from the keyboard, include:

1. Press Alt to select the Control-menu box. Then press Enter (or the up or down cursor key) to display the Control menu.

2. The Move command is already selected; press Enter to engage the Move command. (This causes the pointer to change to two intersecting double-headed arrows.)

3. Press the cursor keys to place the temporary borders of the box into a new location.

4. When the temporary borders are in the desired location, press the Enter key.

Dialog Boxes

Dialog boxes typically resemble small windows that appear in the foreground of the desktop to provide information and to request a user response. Dialog boxes are displayed when:

1. the user chooses a command followed by an ellipsis (...). (For example, choosing the FILE-Exit Windows... command displays the Exit Windows dialog box.)

2. additional information is needed to complete a requested command (such as entering the name of a file to be saved).

3. Windows provides a warning message (i.e., quitting an application before saving a new or revised file contained within the application).

4. Windows provides a message explaining why a requested command cannot be completed (i.e., not having the required hardware (such as a modem) needed to run an application).

The majority of the dialog boxes require input on a limited number of decisions (like the Exit Windows dialog box, which asks you to choose either the OK or Cancel button). Other dialog boxes, such as the Desktop dialog box shown in Figure 2.7, may be a little more complex. In the following pages you

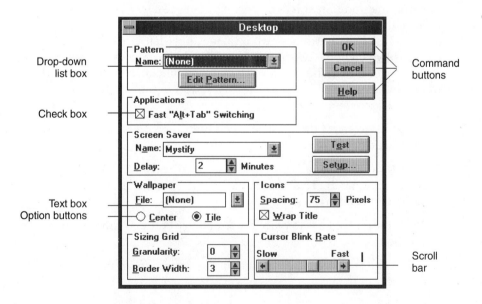

Figure 2.7   The Desktop dialog box.

will learn how to use the Desktop dialog box to control the appearance of your desktop. After learning to work with the elements in the Desktop dialog box, you will be prepared to work with the other Windows dialog boxes.

All dialog boxes contain one or more buttons; many contain lists of choices and areas for entering text. Other common characteristics of dialog boxes include:

- The dialog boxes containing title bars may be moved to any location on the desktop.

- The borders cannot be used for sizing the dialog box.

- Closing dialog boxes (without taking any action) may be accomplished by choosing the Cancel button, pressing Esc, or pressing Alt+F4.

- Most have a Control-menu box which allows the Control menu to be accessed by pressing Alt or clicking on the Control-menu box.

  Complete the following steps to display the Desktop dialog box.

1 With the Program Manager active, display the Main window. Then double-click on the Control Panel icon, in the Main window, to display the Control Panel window.

Your Control Panel window may appear similar to the one in Figure 2.8. Depending upon how your hardware has been configured, you should be viewing 11–13 icons. (If Windows is running in the 386 enhanced mode, a 386 enhanced icon will appear. An installed network will cause the Network icon to appear.)

2 Double-click on the Desktop icon, inside the Control Panel window, to load the module. Your desktop should be similar to the one shown in Figure 2.7.

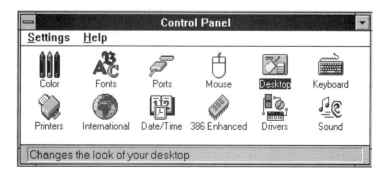

Figure 2.8 The Control Panel window.

The following sections describe some of the common elements found in dialog boxes. The exercise following these sections will provide an opportunity to practice using the various elements in a dialog box.

Command Buttons

Command buttons are used to direct a dialog box to perform a specific action. The buttons are commonly displayed across the top or middle, or down the right side of the box. When you choose (point on and click) a button, you initiate the action listed on the button.

The three buttons located in the upper-right corner of the Desktop dialog box are also commonly found in other dialog boxes. The commands associated with the buttons are described below.

OK: Once your settings are correct, choose this button to initiate the desired action.

Cancel: Choose this button to close the dialog box without taking any action (or press Esc or Alt+F4).

Help: Choose this button (or press Alt+H) to activate the Help menu corresponding with the dialog box.

NOTE: Pointing and clicking with the mouse is the most common way to select any of the dialog box elements. Windows uses one of the following methods to indicate that an element has been selected:

1. surrounding the name of the element with a dotted rectangle, to indicate that once you point and click on the element (or press the Enter key), this element will be engaged.

2. placing a blinking vertical line in a box that contains a line of text.

3. displaying the text inside a box in reverse video.

Keyboard users may select different elements by pressing:

1. Tab to move the selection cursor forward one position.

2. Shift+Tab to move back one position.

3. Alt+ the underlined letter of the element name. For example, when in the Desktop dialog box, press Alt+F to select the File box in the Wallpaper frame. (The names of many, but not all, dialog box elements include an underlined letter that may be used in combination with the Alt key to select the element.)

TIP:

Many dialog boxes are used to ask for confirmation of a requested command (i.e., exiting Windows). When these boxes are first displayed, the OK or Yes button is often surrounded by a dotted rectangle to indicate that pressing Enter will activate the command. If your hands are already on the keyboard, you may prefer to simply press the Enter key, instead of moving a hand from the keyboard to move the mouse and then press the mouse button.

Check Boxes

Some dialog box options can be turned on or off through the use of check boxes. In Figure 2.7, the Applications frame of the Desktop dialog box contains a **check** box with the option turned on. (The "X" in the box, preceding the phrase Fast "Alt + Tab" Switching, indicates that the option is turned on. An empty box means the option is turned off.)

To change the status of the check box, click on the box. If an option appears gray or dimmed, the option is not appropriate for the current situation and cannot be selected.

Option Buttons

The Wallpaper frame contains two option buttons (the small circles next to the words "Center" and "Tile"). **Option buttons** are always grouped as a set of choices and usually displayed within a frame. Only one option in a group may be selected. An option is selected by clicking on it. This will cause the circle in front of the selected option to display a dot. (In Figure 2.7, the Tile option has been selected.)

Text Boxes

Text boxes may be defined as boxes in which you enter information that is used to execute a command. The Wallpaper frame contains the File text box.

To make an entry into a text box, the box must first be selected. If the user presses Tab to select the box, the contents of the text box are highlighted (the text appears in reverse video). Then the desired information may be keyed into the text box. The selected text will be deleted when the user presses the first key of the new information.

There are a few things to remember when using the pointer to select a text box.

1. The pointer changes shape to resemble the end-view of an I-beam when it is placed inside a text box. When you see the I-beam in the text box, click the mouse button to select the text box. The text box cursor appears as a blinking vertical line. The blinking line is referred to as the insertion point and indicates the location where the first character, entered from the keyboard, will be placed in the text box.

TIP:

2. Once you have clicked on a text box, look to see if the existing text is highlighted before entering new information. If the text is not highlighted, your new entry will be merged with the existing one.

3. If the text in the text box is not highlighted

   a. Drag the pointer across the text to select the existing entry. (Don't worry about dragging the pointer past the end of the dialog box. When you release the button only the selected text, within the text box, is highlighted.)

   b. Release the mouse button, and enter the desired information.

NOTE: The Wallpaper File text box is a special type of text box because it can also be treated as a drop-down list box. Drop-down list boxes are discussed shortly.

List Boxes

A **list box** appears in a dialog box as a rectangular frame that displays a list of options. The top half of the Task List dialog box contains a list box showing the names of the open programs. Scroll bars appear along the border of the list box when more options are available than can be displayed in the frame. When your desired option appears in the box, select it by pointing on it and clicking. This usually places the selected option at the top of the list, or enters it into an accompanying text box.

Drop-Down List Boxes

A **drop-down list box** is composed of a single-line text box located next to an underlined down arrow button. Clicking on the down arrow button displays a drop-down list of options that may be selected. (Selecting an option inserts it into the text box.) The *Pattern* frame of the Desktop dialog box (upper left portion of the box) contains the Name drop-down list box. In Figure 2.7, the current choice of "(None)" is displayed. The Screen Saver frame also contains a Name drop-down list box.

NOTE: A **screen saver** displays an everchanging pattern of images on the desktop. With some monitors, continually displaying the same image will burn the image into the screen. When this happens, a *ghost* of the image will constantly appear on your screen. When your screen saver is displayed, you may return to the Windows desktop by moving the mouse or pressing a key. To temporarily turn off the screen saver, set the delay time to zero. To permanently turn off the screen saver, choose (None) in the Name drop-down list box.

Scroll Bars

Along with indicating that a box or window contains more information than is currently visible, scroll bars may also be used in dialog boxes to choose a value on a sliding scale (such as desired speeds or amounts). For example, when working in the Cursor Blink Rate frame of the Desktop dialog box, moving the scroll box to the left or right will change the cursor blink rate.

Dialog Box Exercise

Practice using some of the elements found in the Desktop dialog box by completing the following exercise. (Make sure you start with the Desktop dialog box displayed on your screen.)

1. Press the Tab key until you have selected all the elements in the dialog box at least once. As the elements are selected, look for the highlighted text, or the dotted rectangle around the buttons and boxes.

2. Press the Tab key to select the Cancel button in the upper-right portion of the dialog box. (Remember, pressing Shift+Tab moves the selection cursor backwards.) Then press Enter to close the box.

3   Display the Desktop dialog box by double-clicking on the Desktop icon in the Control Panel window.

4   The Delay text box (inside the Screen Saver frame) is a special type of text box because it accepts input from the keyboard or numbers placed in the box by clicking on the up or down arrows next to the text box.

   Point on the beginning of the Delay text box and drag the pointer across the entry in the box to select the text (the text will then appear highlighted).

   Enter the number 4 on top of the highlighted text to indicate that you want the delay to last 4 minutes. Then click on the down arrow, next to the Delay text box, to reduce the time delay to 2 minutes (the Windows default setting).

5   Click on the down arrow of the Screen Saver Name drop-down list box to display the names of the screen savers supplied with Windows.

6   Move the tip of the pointer onto the Mystify option and click once to select it. Notice how the drop-down list closes as soon as a selection is made. (If the Mystify option has already been chosen, choose a different screen saver.)

7   To see how the screen saver will appear on your screen, choose the Test button, located inside the Screen Saver frame. After a few seconds, move the mouse to return to the Windows desktop.

   Try testing the other screen savers. When you find the one you like best, select it and move to the next step.

8   Move the pointer into the Pattern frame and click on the down arrow button in the Name drop-down list box. This should display a list box containing various pattern choices. Your screen may look similar to Figure 2.9.

9   Use the scroll bar to move toward the bottom of the list, then select the Waffle option.

TIP: When you know the name of the option you want to select in a long drop-down list, most drop-down list boxes allow you to enter the first letter of the name to reach the desired area of the list more quickly. Because the options are in alphabetical order, you will move to the first word starting with the letter you pressed. To leave a list box, without making a choice, move the pointer outside the box, into a blank area of the dialog box, and click once.

10   Continue working in the Pattern Name drop-down list box by clicking on the down arrow button to display the list again. Scroll to the end of the list. Note the existence of the Thatches and Tulip options, then choose the Scottie option.

   With the Scottie option highlighted in the Name text box, enter the letter "T" from the keyboard to display the Thatches option. Press "T" again to display the Tulips option.

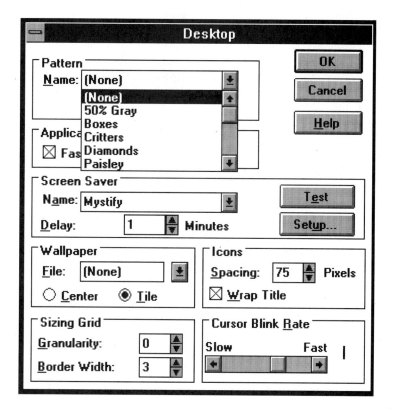

Figure 2.9 The Desktop dialog box Pattern Name drop-down list box.

The "Pattern" frame also includes an Edit Pattern... button that is dedicated for use within this section. Notice that the words are followed by an ellipsis, which indicates that a dialog box will appear when the button is chosen. This dialog box enables the user to view a small sample of the chosen pattern.

11   Click on the Edit Pattern... button to view how the chosen pattern will appear on the desktop.

12   When the Desktop-Edit Pattern dialog box is displayed, notice that the sample box shows how the desktop background will appear and the larger box, in the center, lets you see the pattern of dots used to make an image.

TIP: You may design your own pattern by placing the pointer in the center box and clicking the mouse button at various locations. This either fills or empties the particular dot location. As you change the pattern, the box on the left shows how your new pattern will appear on the desktop. To return a pattern to its original layout, choose the Cancel button in the Desktop-Edit Pattern dialog box.

13   Click on the down arrow to display the drop-down list of patterns and select a pattern name to see how it will appear on the screen. Repeat this step to view a few patterns.

14   Select the Spinner pattern and choose the OK button inside the Desktop-Edit Pattern dialog box. This will close that dialog box and place the word Spinner in the Pattern Name text box of the Desktop dialog box. Your current desktop will not change because you have not left the Desktop dialog box yet. (If you are already using the Spinner pattern, choose a different pattern so that you will see a change when you close the Desktop dialog box.)

15   Move the pointer into the Cursor Blink Rate frame. Drag the scroll box in either direction and note the rate change of the blinking line to the right of the bar.

16   When you are satisfied with the rate of the blinking cursor, and your other settings, choose the OK button of the Desktop dialog box to close the box and establish your new screen saver, desktop pattern, and cursor blink rate.

This concludes the discussion of basic dialog box operations and the Desktop dialog box. Before changing any of the other features of your desktop, read the following section on the Windows Help facility. Then display the Desktop dialog box and review its corresponding Help sections.

Working with the Help Facility

The **Help facility** functions as an *electronic program manual* that is instantly available whenever you see a HELP menu bar choice or a Help button. Most Windows applications include their own on-line Help facility. For example, there are many different Help programs in Windows, such as Program Manager Help, Control Panel Help, and Write Help. When you access the Help facility, you receive detailed information on the current application's procedures and commands.

There are a number of ways to use Help, including:

• viewing a table of contents of the application's basic operations and commands;

- searching on a keyword;

- using the Bookmark command to flag topics of key interest;

- writing your own comments/instructions for a topic using the Annotate feature;

- copying text from a Help topic into another application; and

- providing a hard copy of the Help text through the use of a Print command.

To access the Help facility, use one of the following techniques (some methods will not work in certain situations):

1. Choose HELP, from the application window menu bar, to display the Help drop-down menu, then choose the desired option.

2. Press F1.

3. Choose the Help button in a dialog box (to obtain help for that dialog box).

4. (For some applications) use the cursor keys to select a command on a drop-down menu, then press F1 to view the Help section for that command.

Program Manager is used here to demonstrate how to use a typical application's Help facility. If, by the end of this section, the topic of your choice is not covered, use the Help facility to learn more about it.

The HELP menu is normally located at the end of the application's menu bar. The Program Manager HELP drop-down menu is shown in Figure 2.10. The commands on the menu follow.

Command	Function
Contents	Displays the contents of the current Help facility.
Search for Help On...	Enables the user to locate information on a specific topic.
How to Use Help	Provides instructions for using the Help facility.
Windows Tutorial	Activates an on-screen tutorial explaining basic Windows procedures.
About (*name of application*)...	(In this case, About Program Manager), displays a dialog box showing copyright and licensing information and (in most cases) how the computer resources are being utilized.

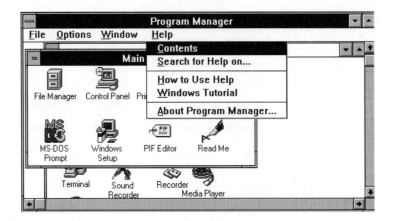

Figure 2.10   The Program Manager HELP drop-down menu.

For the majority of applications, the HELP menu consists of the Contents, Search for Help On..., How to Use Help, and About (*name of application*)... commands. Some programs, like the Program Manager, may include additional items on the HELP menu (such as the Windows Tutorial command).

The Help Window

Choosing the **HELP-Contents command** from the application's menu bar will display the initial window of the program's Help facility. (The initial window of Program Manager Help is shown in Figure 2.11.)

The menu bar, inside the Program Manager Help window, indicates that this is an application window. Therefore, you will be able to size and move the Help window to any location within the desktop. The three key components of the Help window (the menu bar, buttons, and work area) are explained in the following sections.

The Help Menu Bar

The Help menu bar choices include FILE, EDIT, BOOKMARK, and HELP. The commands in the FILE drop-down menu are explained below:

Figure 2.11 The first window of Program Manager Help.

Command	Function
Open	Opens any text file written especially for the Help program.
Print Topic	Prints the current topic in the Help window.
Print Setup	Enables the user to select and set up the printer.
Exit	Closes the Help program.

The commands in the EDIT drop-down menu are:

Copy	Used for copying information from the Help program into another application (via the Windows Clipboard).
Annotate	Used to create your own note to add to a Help topic.

The initial command in the BOOKMARK drop-down menu is:

Define	Used to create your own menu for moving to frequently-referred-to topics in the Help facility. (The first nine bookmarks that are created are listed in the BOOKMARK drop-down menu. When a tenth bookmark is created, a "More" command is added to the menu. Choose the More command to access the remaining bookmarks.)

The commands in the HELP drop-down menu are:

How to Use Help	A brief explanation on how to use Help.
Always on Top	An option for keeping the Help window on top of all other windows.
About Help	Presents a dialog box showing copyright and licensing information and how your computer resources are being utilized.

Complete the following exercise to display the initial Program Manager Help window and to investigate the location of the commands on the drop-down menus.

1 Arrange your desktop to include only the open Program Manager and Main windows.

2 Choose HELP from the menu bar to display the Help drop-down menu. Your desktop may look similar to Figure 2.10.

3 Choose the HELP-Contents command to display the first window of Program Manager Help. Your desktop may look similar to Figure 2.11.

4 Choose each of the words on the Program Manager Help menu bar to display the drop-down menus.

5 Choose the HELP-About Help command to view information regarding your copy of Windows and your computer resources.

6 Choose the OK button (or press Esc) to close the About Help dialog box and return to the initial Program Manager Help window.

Help Buttons

The Help buttons are located just below the Help menu bar (see Figure 2.11). These buttons are found on all the Help programs within Windows 3.1. A brief description of each button's function is listed below.

Button	Function
Contents	Displays the contents of the Help facility.
Search	Enables the user to search for a topic using a keyword.
Back	Displays the previous window.
History	Displays, in last-to-first order, the topics of the windows viewed through the Help program (up to the last 40 topics).
Glossary	Displays a list of defined terms.

Because the Contents button displays the same window you see upon entering the program's Help facility, it is primarily used when you are already viewing a Help topic and need to return to the listing of the program's contents.

When you are not sure how to name the topic you need help with, skim through the contents of the Help facility by looking at the initial Help window. If you know the name of the procedure you are looking for, using the **Search** function allows you to direct Help to display a particular topic in the Help window. Three ways to access the Search command are:

- Enter the application's Help window and choose the Search button.

- Choose the HELP option from the *application's* menu bar, then choose the Search for Help on... command.

- Enter the application's Help window and press ALT+S.

Any of these actions will cause the dialog box shown in Figure 2.12 to be displayed on your desktop.

The following steps describe how to use this dialog box.

1. Place the pointer in the text box above the upper list box and enter the topic of your choice. (Use the backspace key, cursor keys, and the insert and delete keys to edit your entry.) or,

   Scroll through the topics listed in the upper list box and select the desired topic. The topic you select is then placed in the text box.

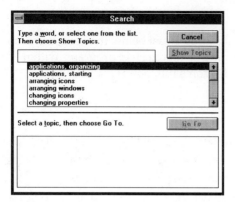

Figure 2.12   The initial Search dialog box in Program Manager Help.

2. Choose the (now active) Show Topics button to see a list of all the topics that relate to the selected concept displayed in the lower list box.

3. Move to the lower list box and select the desired topic (if more than one exists). Then choose the Go To button to move to an explanation of the topic.

   Complete the exercise below to practice using the Search function.

1 Click on the Search button, located in the Program Manager Help window. This displays the Search dialog box and initiates the search process.

2 Use the scroll bar to display the "quitting Windows" topic in the top list box. Select this topic by placing the tip of the pointer on the text and clicking once. This will place the "quitting Windows" topic in the text box near the top of the Search dialog box.

3 Choose the Show Topics button to see the topics relating to the concept of "Quitting Windows" displayed in the lower list box.

4 Because only one topic appears, click on the Go To button to view the text of the "Quitting Windows" topic.

5 Continue working with the Search dialog box by pressing Alt+S. The previous entry in the text box is selected and the vertical blinking line appears at the end of the entry. Enter the word START in the text box and press Enter. (The selected text, in the text box, will be automatically deleted when you begin entering the new topic.)

6 Notice that Windows has modified your term to best match with the topics in the Program Manager Help program. View the various related topics displayed in the lower list box.

TIP: You could have completed steps 5 and 6 by keying the word START and then moving the mouse to choose the Show Topics button. Most people can probably key the topic and press Enter more quickly than keying the topic and choosing the Show Topics button with the mouse. Either technique yields the same results.

7 Select the "Starting an Application from a Group" topic, then choose the Go To button to view the corresponding text.

8 After viewing the "Starting an Application from a Group" text, choose the Search button to return to the Search dialog box.

9 Choose the Show Topics button to redisplay the group of topics relating to "start" in the lower list box. Move the pointer to the lower list box and double-click on the "Starting an Application by Using the Run Command" topic. (Double-clicking on a topic will also move you to its corresponding text.)

10 Leave the current topic on your desktop and read the following paragraphs to prepare for the next exercise.

The functions of the remaining buttons (Back, History, and Glossary) are explained below.

The easiest way to go back one Help window is to choose the Back button. Each time you click on this button (or press Alt+B), you display the previous window in the current Help session.

Choosing the History button does not show your previous Help windows, but it does display the Help History window that lists the previous topics you viewed (see Figure 2.13). (The memory limit of the Help History window is 40 topics. If necessary, size this window to display its enclosed text.) The most

Figure 2.13 The Windows Help History window.

recent topics are at the top of the list. Choose the topic you want to return to by double-clicking on its name.

Choosing the Glossary button reveals the **Glossary window,** which provides a list of terms associated with the application. When a term is selected, its definition appears inside a definition box. (Figure 2.14 displays part of a Glossary window and the definition box for the term "application.") The terms in the Glossary window are the keywords found in the text of the program's Help windows. (In the Help windows, keywords appear underlined and in a color different from normal text.)

To use the Glossary window:

1. Use the window's scroll bar to move through the alphabetical listing until you see the term you want defined.

2. Move the pointer onto the desired word. (Once the pointer is placed on a keyword, it changes shape to look like a hand with the pointer finger extended.)

3. Click on that term to see its definition box.

4. To remove the definition box, click the mouse button.

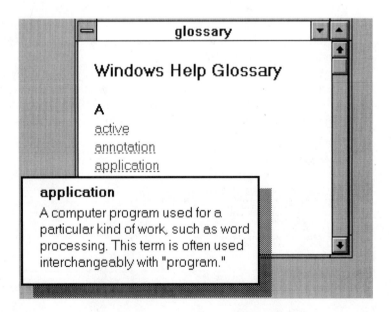

Figure 2.14 The Glossary window and a definition box.

Complete the following exercise to practice using the Back, History, and Glossary buttons.

1 Choose the Back button to review the previous window from the exercise above. (If you followed each of the listed steps you should be viewing the "Starting an Application from a Group" text.

2 Choose the History button to review the topics you have viewed so far. Your list may look similar to the one shown in Figure 2.13.

3 Return to the text of the "Quitting Windows" topic by moving into the Windows Help History window and double-clicking on the "Quitting Windows" topic.

4 Choose the Glossary button, and select the term "Restore button." Read its definition and then click the mouse button once to close the definition box.

5 Return to the Glossary scroll bar, select the term "Group Icon," and read its definition. Then close the definition box.

6 Close the Glossary window by double-clicking on the Control-menu box located in the upper-left corner of the Glossary window.

Selecting Topics and Keywords in the Help Window Work Area

The work area of the first Help window usually consists of a title (i.e., Content for Program Manager Help), a brief introduction to the program, a **How To...** section that identifies the major tasks of the program, and a **Commands** section that defines the commands one may choose through using the program's drop-down menus. (See Figure 2.11.) Occasionally, you will find a Help program with one or two additional segments.

When reviewing the topics in either the "How To..." or "Commands" sections you notice that the topics are underlined and displayed in a different shade than that of the section titles. When you move the mouse to an underlined topic, the pointer changes to a hand. This change indicates that when you click the mouse on a topic, the corresponding topic window is then displayed on the desktop. (Pressing the Tab key, an appropriate number of times, enables keyboard users to select the topic of their choice. Once a topic is selected, press Enter to display the topic window.)

Complete the following exercise to practice selecting topics and keywords from the text in the Help windows.

1 Choose the Contents button to display the contents of Program Manager Help.

2 | Move the pointer into the "How To..." section and click on the "Switch Between Applications" topic. This will display another window describing how to switch to other applications.

    This window has borders and scroll bars. Manipulate this window as you would any other window. If necessary, use the scroll bars to view all the information on the topic.

    You probably noticed that in the Switching Between Applications window, the term *Control menu* appeared in a contrasting color and was underlined. This is the way Windows identifies *keywords;* these are defined terms in the Help facility. Clicking on a keyword brings its definition window to the foreground without changing the underlying screen. When you finish reading the definition, click the mouse to remove the definition box and return to your previous window.

3 | Remain in the Switching Between Applications window and click on the keyword phrase "Control menu." (Just before you click, you'll see the pointer change into a hand.)

4 | After reading the definition, click again to remove the definition box.

5 | To return to the beginning of the Program Manager Help contents, choose the Contents button.

6 | Then select the "Start an Application" topic, listed under the "How To..." section.

7 | As you see, some topics require you to make additional choices. Choose "Starting an Application from a Group."

8 | Click on the keyword "group" to view a definition of this term. (We will use this term often in the next chapter.) Click once to remove the box.

9 | Choose the Contents button to return to the beginning of the Help program.

Accessing Help on Help

In the Help facility, just as in most Windows applications, choosing the HELP-How to Use Help command displays information regarding the procedures and commands of the Help facility.

    Upon choosing the HELP-How to use Help command, you will see the "Contents for How to Use Help" window. Work with this window in the same manner as you worked with the Program Manager Help window.

Summary

This chapter concludes our look at basic Windows operations and procedures. Some of the key concepts to remember are listed below.

You may simultaneously run multiple Windows programs. One of the easiest ways to launch a program is to display the group window containing the desired application icon and then double-click on the corresponding icon. Most program windows are manipulated in the same manner as the Program Manager window.

Three ways to determine which programs are open include:

1. Pressing Alt+Esc (holding down the Alt key, while tapping Esc) to redraw an open program window in the foreground each time Esc is pressed. When viewing the desired window, release Alt, to make the window active.

2. Pressing Alt+Tab (holding down the Alt key while tapping Tab) to draw a small box containing an open program name in the center of the desktop. Each time Tab is pressed, a new program name appears in the box. (This is faster than redrawing each window.) When viewing the desired program name, release Alt, to make the window active.

3. Activating the Task List utility by double-clicking on a non-window area of your desktop (or pressing Ctrl+Esc). The Task List dialog box enables you to switch programs, close programs, tile or cascade the open program windows, or neatly arrange the minimized program icons.

Dialog boxes are displayed to provide information and to request user input. Whenever a menu command that includes an ellipsis is chosen, a dialog box will appear before the rest of the command is executed. Common components of dialog boxes include: command and option buttons, list boxes, drop-down list boxes, check boxes, text boxes, and scroll bars. Dialog boxes can be moved; however, they cannot be sized.

An on-screen Help facility is available with most Windows programs. The Help facility is a program designed to show how to use the application. Most Windows-based applications have a Help program that operates in the same manner as the one reviewed in this chapter. Three common ways to activate Help include:

1. Pressing F1.

2. Choosing the HELP command on the application's menu bar and then choosing the desired command from the drop-down menu.

3. Choosing the Help button in a dialog box (or pressing F1).

The first window of the program's Help facility displays the major program topics under two primary headings: the "How To...:" section lists the basic program operations and the "Commands" section lists the menu commands. Clicking on the desired topic displays the content for that choice. When reading the content, underlined words (in a contrasting color) will occasionally appear. These are keywords. Clicking on keywords brings to the foreground a definition box that describes the keyword. Click once to remove the definition box.

The Help program utilizes a number of buttons. Clicking on the Search button is one way to initiate a word (or phrase) search through the contents of the Help program. The Back button redraws the previous window you viewed. Use this button to move backward (one window at a time) to the beginning of the current Help session. Clicking on the History button shows the names of the previous topics (up to 40 topics) you have viewed so far in the current Help session. Click on the name of the desired topic, in the Windows Help History window, to return to that topic window. The Glossary button activates a list of keywords. Click on a keyword to view its definition box.

Applications

All applications start with Windows loaded and the open Program Manager window on the desktop. Upon completing an application, either exit Windows or close all windows except the Program Manager.

Application 1

1. Open the Accessories group window.

2. Open the Write application and size the window so you can still see the top half of the Accessories window. Enter your name, address, and phone number in the Write work area. (For now use the backspace key, insert and delete keys, and cursor control keys to edit your entries. The Write accessory will be covered later in the text.)

3. Leaving the Write window open, open the Paintbrush program. Size the Paintbrush window so you can still see part of the Accessories window. Place the cursor on the left side of the work area, about one-third of the way down. The pointer changes to a dot. At this point, with the mouse button depressed, write your first name, then release the button. (The Paintbrush accessory will also be covered later in the text.)

4. Move back to the Accessories window and open the Calculator program. Move this window to the lower right corner of the desktop.

5. Open the Cardfile, Calendar, and Notepad accessories and place the windows along the lower portion of the desktop.

6. Press the Alt+Esc key combination to cycle through your applications. Using this combination, open the Calculator. Then reduce the Calculator to an icon.

7. Press the Alt+Tab key combination to open the Paintbrush program.

8. Use the Task List utility to Tile your open windows.

9. Use the Task List utility to display your windows in the Cascade format. (If Windows is unable to display all of the open windows in a downward cascade, the active window will be displayed on top of the cascaded windows.)

10. Use the Task List utility to close the Calendar program and to make the Write window active.

11. Switch to Program Manager and try to exit Windows. Choose the Cancel button when seeing the "Exit Windows" dialog box.

12. Reduce all the open windows to icons.

13. Scatter the icons throughout your screen, then rearrange them using Task List.

14. Open the Program Manager window.

15. Click once on the Notepad icon to display its Control menu, then choose Close to close the accessory. Repeat this step with all of the remaining icons (save no files). Then exit Windows.

Application 2

In this application you will print a topic from the Program Manager Help Facility. Use the default printer settings already installed for your system; do not attempt to set up a printer at this time.

1. Open the Program Manager Help Facility.

2. Choose the HELP-Search for Help on... command and complete the necessary steps to display the text for the "quitting Windows" topic.

3. Choose the FILE-Print Topic command to print the text of the "Quitting Windows" topic.

4. Exit Windows.

Application 3

1. Open the Main window, double-click on the Control Panel icon to open the Control Panel window. Then double-click on the Desktop icon (inside the Control Panel window) to display the Desktop dialog box.

2. At the top of the back of the printout from Application 2, write the heading "Original Desktop Dialog Box Settings" and record the current settings of the Desktop dialog box. Then change the settings to customize the desktop to appear the way you would like to work with it during your next Windows session. Choose the OK button to see your new settings in use.

3. Just below the list of the original Desktop dialog box settings, write the title "Desired Desktop Dialog Box Settings" and then record your new settings.

4. Use your initial list of Desktop settings to return the desktop to its previous settings.

5. Exit Windows.

Application 4

1. Open the Calculator program.

2. Open the Help program for Calculator.

3. Browse through the topics listed in the Contents for Calculator Help window. Then click on the "Enter Calculations" topic. Read the instructions for how to use the Calculator and then *use the Calculator* to complete the following problems. Record your answers on the back of the Application 2 printout.

   a. $7 + 8 =$ _____

   b. $74567 - 47762.5 =$ _____

   c. $23 * 37 =$ _____ (The * is used to multiply one number by another.)

   d. $25 / 4 =$ _____ (The / is used to divide one number by another.)

4. Close the Calculator program.

Application 5

1. Choose the Help option on the Program Manager menu bar.

2. Choose the "Windows Tutorial" option and view the information in the tutorial. (This will take approximately 15 minutes.)

3. On the back of the Application 2 printout, list the two most helpful concepts discussed in the tutorial.

3

Program Manager

When you start Windows, you automatically load
one of the two Windows shell programs—Program
Manager or File Manager. Each shell program displays a window from which you conduct your basic
Windows activities, including beginning and ending Windows sessions and launching other programs. Program Manager, the topic of this chapter,
is the more visually oriented shell, as it utilizes
icons to help the user complete many activities. File
Manager, which is discussed in the next two chapters, displays file, directory, and disk drive names
to help the user conduct various tasks.

By completing the first two chapters you have
already gained some experience with the Program
Manager. In this chapter, you will enhance your
knowledge of Program Manager as you learn to:

1. work with the initial group windows provided
   by Windows.

2. create and organize new group windows and
   program-item icons.

Group Windows

Grouping related applications together is a key feature of the Program Manager. The first thing you will likely see when you load Windows is the Program Manager window containing one or more group windows and a number of group icons located across the lower portion of the Program Manager window (see Figure 3.1).

Each item inside a group window is represented by a program-item icon. Most of the time, the program-item icons have a unique appearance. Double-clicking on an icon starts its corresponding program.

A minimized group window is shown as a group icon near the bottom of the Program Manager window. All group icons look alike (similar to a file folder displaying two rows of symbols). However, each group icon has a unique label below its symbol.

Initial Groups Created When Windows Is Installed

Depending upon the installation procedure used, Windows creates four or five predefined groups when it is installed. These groups are discussed below.

Main Group

The Windows system applications, located in the Main group window (see Figure 3.1), are used to control the Windows environment and manage the computer's resources. Items in the Main group window include:

File Manager: the second shell program that, along with launching other applications and starting and ending the Windows sessions, allows for managing files and directories on hard drives, file servers, and floppy disks.

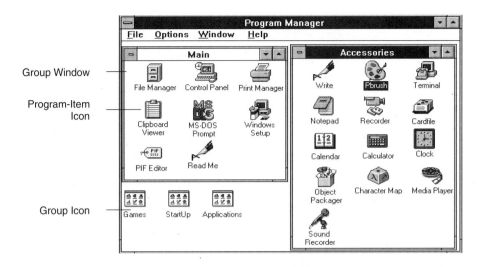

Figure 3.1 The Program Manager window displaying the Main and Accessories group windows and the Games, StartUp, and Applications group icons.

Control Panel: the program that controls your Windows environment, including the look of your screen elements, what fonts and printers are available, and the use of various hardware components.

Print Manager: the program that manages the printing requests from Windows applications. Non-Windows programs do not use the Print Manager.

Clipboard Viewer: a short-term storage area used for transferring information between applications.

MS-DOS Prompt: the avenue to access DOS. Double-click on the icon to enter DOS. Type EXIT at the DOS prompt to return to Windows.

Windows Setup: the program used to change system settings, set up applications, and add/remove optional Windows components.

PIF Editor: the program used to modify Program Information Files (PIF's) for non-Windows applications. (If your Windows 3.1 was upgraded from Windows 3.0, the PIF Editor has remained in the Accessories group.)

Read Me: a series of notes to read before you start using Windows.

Accessories Group

The programs in the Accessories group (see Figure 3.1) can be viewed as a set of Windows desktop productivity tools. The Accessories group includes:

Write: an easy-to-use, Windows-based word processing program that allows you to perform fundamental word processing tasks.

Paintbrush: a paint program used to create figures and images.

Terminal: a telecommunications tool used to connect your computer with other computers (via modems).

Notepad: a mini-word processor or text editor used for creating short messages; can also be used to edit ASCII text files.

Recorder: a tool to record your Windows macros. (A macro is a series of keystrokes that are executed in a predefined order when an assigned key combination is pressed.)

Cardfile: an electronic notecard organizer.

Calendar: a daily/monthly appointment manager.

Calculator: displays either a standard electronic calculator or a scientific calculator.

Clock: a tool to display the current date and time.

Object Packager: a tool used to insert an icon that represents an embedded or linked object into a file.

Character Map: a tool used to insert symbols and special characters into documents.

Media Player: a tool to control your system's multimedia hardware.

Sound Recorder: a tool that allows for the playing, recording, and editing of sound files (once a sound card is added to your system).

Games Group

Two games come with the Windows package (see Figure 3.2):

Solitaire: an electronic version of the single-player card game.

Minesweeper: an electronic minefield, where the user is challenged to locate the mines before causing one to explode.

Many more games may be purchased through various vendors.

StartUp Group

This window contains applications that start whenever Windows is loaded. In Figure 3.2, the Calendar, Clock, and Calculator icons are located within the StartUp window, indicating that these programs are automatically loaded when the Windows program is started.

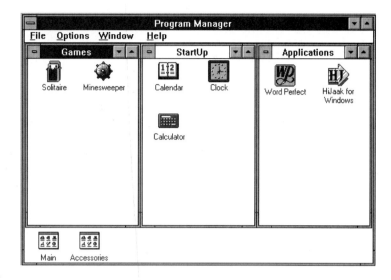

Figure 3.2 The Program Manager window displaying the Games, StartUp, and Applications windows.

Any number of applications can be placed in this group. This group is empty when Windows is first installed. To use this feature, the user must add the desired applications to the group window. Then, the next time Windows is loaded, those applications start along with Windows.

TIP: If you do not want to launch the applications in the StartUp window when Windows is loaded, depress the Shift key after entering the command to start Windows. Keep the Shift key depressed until the Windows 3.1 logo is removed from the screen.

Applications Group

The purpose of the Applications group window is to display the program-item icons for the programs you would like to access through Windows. For example, in Figure 3.2 the Applications window contains the program-item icons for "WordPerfect" and "Hijaak for Windows."

During the **Express Setup** procedure (which is the standard method used to install Windows), the more common applications that are already on the hard drive are automatically placed in the Applications group window. When the **Custom Setup** procedure is used, the installer is given a choice regarding the creation of an Applications group and how Windows should work with the desired applications.

Creating and Removing Groups

You may create as many groups (and corresponding) windows as needed to organize your applications in the way that makes the most sense to you. After creating a new group window you may add new program-item icons or move or copy existing program-item icons into the window. When a program-item icon appears in more than one window, only the icon and the command line needed to launch the program are duplicated in your Windows files (the entire software program is not duplicated). When you no longer need a group, delete it. Deleting a group does not delete the actual applications in the group; you are removing only the pathways to the applications that were residing in the group window.

To learn the steps needed to create a group window, complete the following exercise. (Although it is not required, before starting the exercise you may want to organize your desktop by minimizing any open group windows inside the Program Manager window.)

1 Display the Program Manager window, then choose the FILE-New... command. This action displays the New Program Object dialog box, shown in Figure 3.3.

2 If it is not already selected, select the Program Group option by clicking on the phrase or its option button. Then choose the OK button to display the Program Group Properties dialog box (see Figure 3.4).

3 To name your new group window "Additional Group," key the phrase "Additional Group" in the Description text box. (Use the cursor control keys, the backspace, and delete keys to edit any mistakes. Do not press Enter yet.)

NOTE: You may enter a total of 30 characters and spaces in the Description text box. Generally, you benefit by using short, descriptive names for your windows, as these names are placed under the group window icon.

If desired, you may enter a one- to eight-character filename in the Group File text box. Program Manager automatically uses a GRP extension, so do not

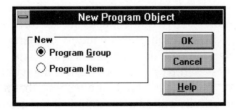

Figure 3.3 The New Program Object dialog box.

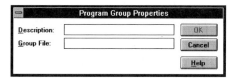

Figure 3.4 The Program Group Properties dialog box.

enter your own extension. This becomes the name of the DOS file Program Manager uses to record information about the program group. If you do not enter a filename, Program Manager creates its own name by using the first eight characters you entered in the Description text box.

4 For this exercise, do not make an entry in the Group File text box. Press Enter, or choose the OK button to view the new Additional Group group window.

5 Reduce your new window to an icon by clicking on its minimize button.

6 Find your new group icon. (It is probably located in the lower portion of the Program Manager window). Note that more than one line may be used to display its title.

7 Open the WINDOW menu and view the lower portion of the drop-down menu to see the listing of the original groups and the new one just created. Click on the Additional Group name to open the new window.

Sometimes you may need to rename a group window. The steps for this procedure are listed below:

1. Reduce the desired window to a group icon.

2. Click once on the desired group icon to select it.

3. Choose the FILE-Properties... command to display the Program Group Properties dialog box containing the current group information.

4. Key the new group name into the Description text box and choose the OK button.

TIP: If the window to be renamed is empty, it need not be reduced to an icon. Make the window active and complete steps 3 and 4.

NOTE: Although the name of the group window may be changed in the Program Group Properties dialog box, the original Group File filename (the file Windows uses to record group information) will remain the same unless you change it yourself.

In the exercise below, you will delete the Additional Group window as a way to learn the steps needed for removing group windows.

1 The desired group window should first be reduced to an icon. Therefore, minimize the Additional Group window to display its group icon.

NOTE: When you delete a group window you automatically delete the program-item icons located inside the window.

2 Click once on the Additional Group icon to select it. (Disregard the group's Control menu, if it appears when you select the icon.)

3 Choose the FILE-Delete command (or press the Delete key). The Delete dialog box (a "safety net") appears, asking for confirmation for deleting the group.

4 Choose the Yes button to delete the group.

NOTE: You may delete an open *empty* group window by making sure it is the active window and then completing steps 3 and 4. An open, active window containing one or more program-item icons always displays a selected program-item icon. Therefore, when the FILE-Delete command is chosen, Windows responds with a dialog box, asking if the selected *program-item icon* is to be deleted.

While deleting a group is a simple process, it pays to be careful during this process. The only file that is deleted is the .GRP file; however, if you delete a group by mistake, you have to rebuild it.

Customizing Program Groups

It's natural for your computing needs to change over time. Along with being able to create your own groups, it is beneficial to know how to modify the groups when your needs change. In the exercises below, you will place various program-item icons into new and existing group windows. This will allow you to launch the corresponding applications from a variety of locations. Although many of these tasks can be accomplished using the keyboard, we will focus on using the mouse.

Adding a Program to a Group

If you add a new software package to your system after Windows has been installed, you may want to add the new program to an existing group. In the following exercise you will use the FILE-New... command to create a duplicate calculator icon, give it a new name (to represent a new program added to your hard drive), and then add the new icon to the Accessories window.

1   Open the Accessories group window and select (click once on) the Calculator icon (the word Calculator will appear in reverse video when it is selected).

2   Choose the FILE-New... command to display the New Program Object dialog box (see Figure 3.3). Select the Program Item option and then choose OK.

3   When the Program Item Properties dialog box appears (see Figure 3.5), key in the name Practice Windows Calc in the Description text box. Do *not* press Enter.

4   Move to the Command Line text box by either selecting it with the mouse or pressing the Tab key. Key the filename and extension CALC.EXE. This file starts the newly named program. If the CALC.EXE file is not in the current directory path, you will need to list the proper path before entering the filename and extension.

NOTE: If you cannot remember the name of the file (or its path) needed to start a program, choose the Browse... button to view the Browse dialog box (see Figure 3.6). The Windows default setting for the Browse dialog box is to display all files (in the selected directory) with an .EXE, .PIF, .COM, and .BAT extension. Files with .EXE and .COM are commonly used to start programs. Files with a .PIF extension are used by Windows to work with non-Windows programs. BAT files are batch files that usually consist of a number of commands that execute at the DOS level.

    The basic procedure for using the Browse dialog box is listed below:

1. Select the desired drive from the Drives drop-down list box.

2. Double-click on the desired directory shown in the Directories list box. (Make sure that a shaded, *open* file folder is displayed in front of the directory you have chosen—the directory and file icon should appear highlighted. While many folders may appear open, only the selected folder will appear in a shaded and open format in the list box.)

Figure 3.5 The Program Item Properties dialog box.

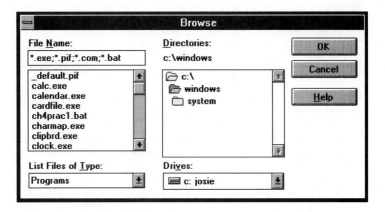

Figure 3.6 The Browse dialog box.

3. Select the desired file in the File Name list box. (This displays the name of the selected file in the File Name text box.)

4. Choose the OK button (or press Enter) to close the Browse dialog box. The path and selected file are automatically placed in the Command Line text box of the Run dialog box. (Double-clicking on the desired filename in step 3 automatically closes the Browse dialog box and places the file and path in the Command Line text box of the Run dialog box.)

5 This concludes our entries into the dialog box. Choose the OK button. (For the purposes of this exercise, if a dialog box appears with the warning that the path you listed may not be available at a later time, just choose the Yes button to continue.)

Completion of this step displays a second Calculator icon in the Accessories window. The new Calculator icon displays the title Practice Windows Calc below it. (Depending on the size of your Accessories window, you may need to resize the window, or use its scroll bars, to see the additional icon.)

NOTE: Optional steps not included in the preceding exercise with the Program Item Properties dialog box include:

1. In the Working Directory text box, enter the location where the application's program files (and any new files) are stored. When the application is running, the directory specified here becomes the current directory.

2. When this application is running you may use a shortcut key combination to make it active. To do this, move to the Short Key text box and choose a key to be pressed in combination with the Alt and Ctrl keys. After pressing the desired key—the text line shows the Alt and Ctrl keys, along with the key you entered.

3. To reduce the application to an icon when it is first started, click on the Run Minimized check box. (This is normally done when you need a background program to be quickly available when you run another program.)

Adding DOS Program Items to a Group

Most Windows applications have a corresponding icon, such as the Calculator icon in the previous exercise. The Windows package includes numerous unassigned icons when it is first installed. Some of the icons are designed for popular non-Windows programs, such as the DOS version of WordPerfect. There is also a generic icon that may be used for less popular DOS-based applications. Although many DOS-based applications may use the same icon, the description below each icon helps to quickly identify the corresponding programs.

In the previous exercise above, you added a new program item to the Accessories group window. The program you added was a Windows-based program that was (most likely) located in the Windows directory. In the steps below, you will place two non-Windows programs, which are not located in the standard Windows directory, in the Accessories window. To complete these steps, you will need to use your *Using Microsoft Windows 3.1* Data Disk.

1 If the Accessories group window is not already open, open it and make sure it is the active window.

2 Choose the FILE-New... command to view the New Program Object dialog box. Select the Program Item option, then choose the OK button.

3 When the Program Item Properties dialog box appears, key in the name Chapter 3 Practice App #1 in the Description text box. Do *not* press Enter.

4 Move to the Command Line text box and enter the drive letter, file-name, and extension needed to start the CH3PRAC1.BAT program. (Key A:CH3PRAC1.BAT if your Data Disk is in drive A.)

5 Because no other modifications are needed in the rest of the dialog box, press Enter (or choose OK).

If a dialog box warning that the path you listed may not be available at a later time appears, choose Yes to continue.

6 An icon looking like a computer monitor with the letters MS DOS on the screen and the description "Chapter 3 Practice App #1" below it should now appear in the Accessories window.

7 Repeat the above steps using the CH3PRAC2.BAT file on your Data Disk. Describe the program as "Chapter 3 Practice App #2." Depending on the size of your Accessories window, you may need to enlarge the window to see the newly added icons. Leave the Accessories window open and continue with the next section.

Assigning Different Icons

If you are not satisfied with the icon Program Manager assigns to your program, you can assign a new one. Program Manager normally has a variety of unassigned icons from which to choose. Follow the steps below to change the icon for the Chapter 3 Practice App #2 program.

|1| If the Chapter 3 Practice App #2 icon in the Accessories window is not already selected, open the Accessories window and select the Chapter 3 Practice App #2 icon.

|2| Choose the FILE-Properties... command. When the Program Item Properties dialog box appears, click on the Change Icon button. A dialog box tells you that no icons exist for the program and that you may choose one of the icons in Program Manager to represent the selected program. Click on OK to see the various icons to choose from in the Change Icon dialog box.

|3| Scroll through the icons until you find one that you want to use. Click on the desired icon to select it and then click on the OK button.

|4| You should now be viewing the Program Item Properties dialog box again. Look in the lower left corner of the box to view the icon you just selected. If you are satisfied with your choice, click on OK.

Moving Program Items to Other Groups

In the following exercise you will create a new group window, and then move three program-item icons from the Accessories window into your new window.

|1| Make a new group window titled "Chapter 3 Practice." (Leave this window open and move to step 2.)

|2| Open the Accessories window.

|3| Move the Chapter 3 Practice App #1 icon from the Accessories window into the Chapter 3 Practice window by:

a. Placing the pointer on the Chapter 3 Practice App #1 icon.

b. Depressing the mouse button and dragging the icon into the Chapter 3 Practice window.

TIP: You may want to use the Window-Tile command, from the Program Manager menu bar, to arrange your group windows.

4   Move the Chapter 3 Practice App #2 and Practice Windows Calc icons into the Chapter 3 Practice window.

5   With the Chapter 3 Practice window active, choose the Arrange Icons command from the WINDOW menu to neatly organize your icons.

6   Minimize the Chapter 3 Practice window.

Copying Program Items to Other Groups

Windows allows you to move or copy program-item icons into open or minimized windows.

In the following exercise you will copy the icons of various Windows Accessories into the minimized Chapter 3 Practice window.

1   Start with the Accessories window open (with no scroll bars) and the Chapter 3 Practice window minimized.

2   Position the pointer on the Clock icon in the Accessories window.

3   Press and hold down the Ctrl key, then use the mouse to drag a duplicate Clock icon on top of the Chapter 3 Practice group window icon. When the duplicate icon is on top of the Chapter 3 group icon, release the mouse button, then release the Ctrl key.

4   Repeat steps 2 and 3 to copy the Sound Recorder and the Object Packager from the Accessories window into the Chapter 3 Practice window.

5   Open the Chapter 3 Practice group window to see the results of your efforts.

6   Activate the Clock program in the Chapter 3 Practice window, by double-clicking on it, to see that you can run the accessory from a different window. Then close the Clock program.

Deleting Program Items from a Group

Deleting a program item from a group window is similar to deleting an entire group. Complete the following exercise to remove the Sound Recorder and Object Packager icons from the Chapter 3 Practice window.

1   Select the Sound Recorder icon inside of the Chapter 3 Practice window.

2   Press the Delete key (or choose the Delete command from the FILE menu).

$\boxed{3}$ Choose Yes in the Delete dialog box.

$\boxed{4}$ Repeat steps 1–3 to remove the Object Packager icon from the Chapter 3 Practice window.

   To conclude the group window exercises, you will delete the Chapter 3 Practice group window with some program-item icons still in it.

$\boxed{1}$ Minimize the Chapter 3 Practice group window.

$\boxed{2}$ Click once on the Chapter 3 Practice group icon to select it.

$\boxed{3}$ Choose the FILE-Delete command.

$\boxed{4}$ Choose Yes in the Delete dialog box to delete the Chapter 3 Practice group.

The OPTIONS Menu

The Program Manager OPTIONS menu includes three commands: Auto Arrange, Minimize on Use, and Save Settings. Each command may be turned on or off by opening the OPTIONS menu and selecting the command. A checkmark placed in front of the command, indicates the command has been turned on; a command appearing without a checkmark indicates the command is turned off.

   The Auto Arrange command rearranges the group window's program-item icons whenever icons have been moved or added to the window, or the size of the window has been modified. The Minimize on Use command (previously mentioned in Chapter 2) minimizes the Program Manager window whenever you start an application. The Save Settings command saves the current size and position of the group windows for your next Windows session.

TIP: After you have initially used the Save Settings command, you may want to turn the command off. Then, any changes you make in subsequent sessions will not replace your desired settings.

Quitting Program Manager When Other Applications Are Open

If Program Manager is your default shell, quitting Program Manager exits you from Windows. If there are open Windows applications, containing no unsaved files, the applications close when you close Program Manager. If the latest modifications to documents have not been saved, a "safety net" message appears warning you to save your files before closing Program Manager. Program Manager does not close any non-Windows applications that have been started through Windows. To exit these programs, you need to return to the non-Windows application and use the appropriate exit procedure. Exiting a non-Windows application that has been started from Windows returns you to the Windows shell program.

Summary

In this chapter we discussed some of the major aspects of the Program Manager shell. Some of the key points of the chapter are listed below.

Program Manager is the default Windows shell from which you start and finish your Windows sessions and launch your various applications.

When Windows is initially installed the Main, Accessories, Games, StartUp, and (usually) Applications group windows are created.

Programs are placed in groups as a matter of convenience. It is easy to create your own program groups; therefore, you do not need to stay with the groups supplied when you first install Windows.

To create a new group:

1. Choose the FILE-New... command.

2. Select Program Group in the New Program Object dialog box; click on OK.

3. Enter the name of the group in the Description text box of the Program Group Properties dialog box.

4. Choose OK.

To delete a group:

1. Minimize the group window and make sure it is selected.

2. Choose the FILE-Delete command.

3. Click on Yes to confirm the group deletion.

Add a program to a group by placing its icon in the group window. A program-item icon may be added to as many windows as needed. When an icon is placed in more than one window, only the icon (and its pathway to the corresponding program) is being reproduced. The actual program is not duplicated.

To add a program-item icon to a group window:

1. Open the desired window.

2. Choose the FILE-New... command.

3. Select the Program Item option from the New Program Object dialog box; then choose the OK button.

4. Enter the text used to identify the icon in the Description text box of the Program Item Properties dialog box.

5. Type the path, filename, and extension needed to launch the program in the Command Line text box.

6. (For our general purposes no entries need be made in the remaining text or check boxes.) Choose OK.

   To delete a program from a group:

1. Open the desired group window.

2. Select the icon to be deleted.

3. Press the Delete key (or choose the FILE-Delete command).

4. Click on Yes to confirm the program item deletion.

To **move a program from one group to another,** drag the icon from its current window into the destination window or the group window icon.

To **copy a program into another window,** hold down the Ctrl key while dragging the icon into the desired window or group window icon.

If you use Program Manager as the Windows shell program, you exit Windows when you close Program Manager.

Applications

All of the following applications start with Windows loaded and the Program Manager window open.

Application 1

1. Open the Accessories window.

2. In the Accessories window, create a new program-item icon for a duplicate Calendar program. Use the same Calendar icon, but label the duplicate "Calendar 2."

3. Use a similar procedure to step 2 to create duplicate Calculator and Clock icons. Title these duplicate icons "Calculator 2" and "Clock 2."

Application 2

1. Create a new group window entitled "Chapter 3 Applications."

2. Copy the Calendar 2 and Calculator 2 program-item icons from the Accessories window into the Chapter 3 Applications window.

3. Move the Clock 2 icon from the Accessories Window into the Chapter 3 Applications window.

4. Launch each of the applications in the Chapter 3 Applications window. Once you see that each application is running, use Task List to close the Calendar 2, Calculator 2, and Clock 2 applications.

5. Choose the WINDOW-Arrange Icons command to neatly display the icons in the Chapter 3 Applications window.

6. Delete the Calendar 2 and Calculator 2 icons from the Accessories window.

Application 3

In this application you will learn to use the Notepad accessory to provide a printout showing which group windows contain the program-item icons listed below. (For now, just use the cursor keys, backspace key, and delete key for editing your entries.)

1. Open the Accessories window and double-click on the Notepad icon to open the Notepad accessory.

2. Key your name on the first line, press Enter, then place today's date on the next line and press Enter twice.

3. Create the column headings of PROGRAM-ITEM ICON and GROUP WINDOW on the same line and press Enter.

4. Working from the list below, enter the name of a program-item icon and its corresponding group window underneath the proper headings. (See Figure 3.7 to view an illustration of the partially completed assignment.) Enter the following program-item icons under their corresponding group window on the Notepad: Notepad, Control Panel, Minesweeper, Clock 2, Print Manager, Calendar.

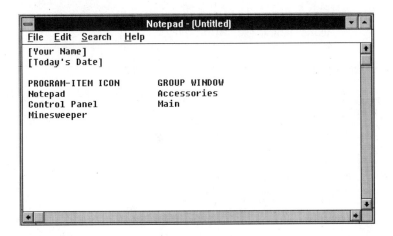

Figure 3.7 Format for Application 3.

5. Print your completed table by choosing the (Notepad) FILE-Print command. (Do not use Page Setup or Print Setup commands yet; you will learn about these commands in later chapters.)

6. Quit the Notepad accessory by choosing the (Notepad) FILE-Exit command. (Do not save your file.)

Application 4

1. Delete the Calendar 2 and the Clock 2 program-item icons from the Chapter 3 Applications window.

2. Close the Chapter 3 Applications window, then delete the window, even though it still contains the Calculator 2 icon.

NOTE: If you are working on a network and mistakenly delete the wrong group window, see your network administrator. You may be asked to rebuild the window using the techniques that were stated earlier in the chapter. The first part of the chapter lists the program items found in each of the Program Manager default groups.

3. Quit Program Manager to end your Windows session.

4

File Manager—Part I

File Manager, the second Windows shell program, helps you manage your files by graphically displaying the organization of the files and directories on your hard drive(s) and floppy disks. Along with being able to start/end your Windows sessions and launch other applications, this powerful application can help you:

- copy, rename, move, delete, locate, and print files.

- create, rename, delete, and copy complete directories.

- format, label, and copy disks and create system disks.

- connect and disconnect from a network file server.

The features of File Manager are discussed in the next two chapters. Chapter 4 focuses on working with the File Manager windows, changing the active drive and directory, and working with the File Manager disk commands. Chapter 5 discusses how File Manager may be used to manipulate your files and directories.

Because of its speed and flexibility, the Windows 3.1 version of File Manager is a major improvement over the Windows 3.0 File Manager.

The Windows and DOS Partnership

As you work through the next two chapters, you will learn many of the File Manager commands used for manipulating files and directories. All of the File Manager commands may also be accomplished by entering their corresponding DOS character-based commands at the DOS prompt. To the relief of millions, the File Manager menu commands and drag-and-drop feature enable users to perform standard file, directory, and disk operations without working with the rigid structure of the DOS character-based commands.

The terms "file" and "directory" are used throughout the text and are defined below:

File: A set of related data (like a program or a document) that has been given a name and stored on a disk.

Directory: A group of related files, located under the same group name. A directory may contain files and other directories (referred to as subdirectories).

When you use File Manager to display the names of the items on your Data Disk, it is helpful to understand the basic DOS naming conventions for files and directories. The key DOS naming conventions are listed below.

1. The name of a file or directory may have two parts: the name (1–8 characters) and an optional extension (1–3 characters). The name and the extension are separated with a period. For instance, the file USINGWIN.CH4 includes the name—USINGWIN—and the extension—CH4.

2. The name or extension may not contain any spaces or include the following characters: . / [ ] ; = " / ; \ ,

3. The * is a DOS wildcard that represents up to eight characters of a name of a file or directory and up to three characters of an extension. The ? is a DOS wildcard that represents one character in the name or extension of a file or directory.

The File Manager Window

Follow the steps below to start File Manager.

1 Load windows and open the Main window.

2 Double-click on the File Manager icon (it looks like a 2-drawer file cabinet) to display the File Manager window.

NOTE: Your desktop may appear similar to the one shown in Figure 4.1. In Figure 4.1, Windows was loaded from the C drive and the File Manager default settings were used to control the appearance of the windows. Don't be concerned if your windows look a little different from the ones in the text. You will soon learn to control how the windows are displayed.

The **File Manager window,** like the Program Manager window (and other application windows), includes a Control-menu box, title bar, sizing buttons, menu bar, work area for document windows and icons, and adjustable borders. The File Manager window may be moved throughout the desktop. The **status bar,** located along the bottom of the window, provides information about the selected drive, including the number of bytes free, total number of bytes used, and number of files.

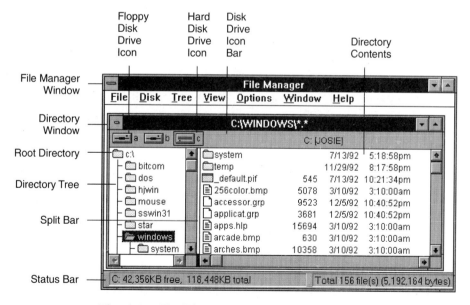

Figure 4.1 The File Manager window and a directory window.

Just as the Program Manager shell has its own special document windows (the group windows), the File Manager shell uses unique document windows, commonly referred to as **directory windows** (see Figure 4.1). Directory windows graphically provide a view of the selected drive's directory and file structure and give a glimpse of your system's other drives.

The top of a directory window contains the common document window elements: the Control-menu box, the title bar, and the sizing buttons. Included in the title bar is the path for the directory being displayed. In Figure 4.1, the path is C:\WINDOWS\; the *.* indicates that all files in the directory are displayed. Scroll bars are often found on directory windows to indicate that more files and directories are included in the window than can currently be displayed. The rest of the directory window is composed of four parts:

- **Disk drive icon bar:** The bar located underneath the title bar, which displays the name of the current disk and an icon for each floppy drive, hard drive, RAM drive, and network drive available to the user.

- **Directory tree:** The left section of the directory window, which displays the structure of the directories of the current disk. The root directory is shown in the upper left corner, with the other directories branching below and to the right of the root (hence the tree concept). The root directory appears as C:\> in Figure 4.1.

- **Directory contents:** The right section of the directory window, which displays the names of the directories and files within the selected directory in the directory tree.

- **Split bar:** The moveable bar that separates the directory tree and the directory contents sections of the window.

Inside the directory window, **selection cursors** appear as rectangles surrounding the most recently selected item from the disk drive icon bar, directory tree, and directory contents section of the window. When a directory is first displayed, only two selection cursors appear—the disk drive and the directory tree cursors; no item in the directory contents section is initially selected. When a selection cursor is active in one portion of the directory window, the remaining selection cursors are inactive. The entry in the active selection cursor appears highlighted (in reverse video). Inactive selection cursors surround the selected entries but do not highlight them. (In Figure 4.1, the active selection cursor surrounds the Windows directory in the directory tree.)

Changing Drives

To view the structure of the contents of a drive, click on its icon in the disk drive icon bar. Figure 4.1 shows three icons, representing the A, B, and C drives. Note the differences between the A and B (floppy) drive icons and the C (hard) drive icon. The rectangle surrounding the C drive icon indicates that the C drive has been selected; therefore, its directory structure appears in the directory tree.

Complete the following steps to view the contents of the drive holding your *Using Microsoft Windows 3.1* Data Disk.

1 The File Manager window should already be displayed from the previous exercise. If not, load Windows, and then start the File Manager program by double-clicking on the File Manager icon in the Main window.

2 Open the VIEW menu on the File Manager menu bar. If a check mark is *not* displayed in front of the All File Details command, select this command. If a check mark appears, close the VIEW menu.

3 Insert the Data Disk into the A drive.

4 Place the tip of the pointer on the A drive icon, in the disk drive icon bar, and click once. An hour glass icon should appear in the area of the pointer and the A drive light should be turned on to indicate that the drive is engaged. After a few seconds, a new directory window should appear. Your window should look similar to the one shown in Figure 4.2.

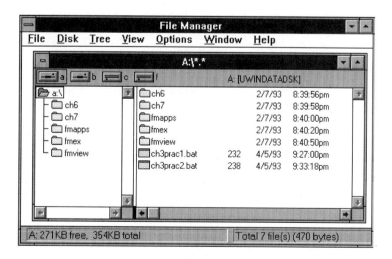

Figure 4.2 The directory window for the root directory of the *Using Microsoft Windows 3.1* Data Disk.

Changing Directories

The purpose of using directories is to place related files into the same location. In this chapter you will work with existing directories and the information displayed in the directory windows. In the next chapter you will learn how to create and remove directories and how to transfer files from one directory to another.

Complete the following exercise to practice working with directory windows. (This exercise starts with the assumption that the directory window for your Data Disk appears on your desktop—this is the point where you concluded the previous exercise. Make sure to display this directory window before starting step 1.)

1 Note that the path of the current directory is listed on the directory window title bar. (In this case, the path is listed as A:*.* —this will change when you complete step 2.) Also notice that the label of the disk (UWINDATADSK) is listed on the disk drive icon bar.

2 When the window for the Data Disk opens, the root directory (A:\) should be selected in the directory tree. Move to the directory tree, place the tip of the pointer on the name (or icon) of the FMVIEW directory and click once. Your new window should appear similar to Figure 4.3.

Notice the changes in the directory window contents sections and title bar. Then look at the directory tree to see that the icon for the FMVIEW directory has changed to an *open* file folder to indicate it is the current directory.

3 In the directory tree section, click on the icon for the root directory (A:\) and note the changes in the title bar and contents section. (Your window should now look like it did in step 1.)

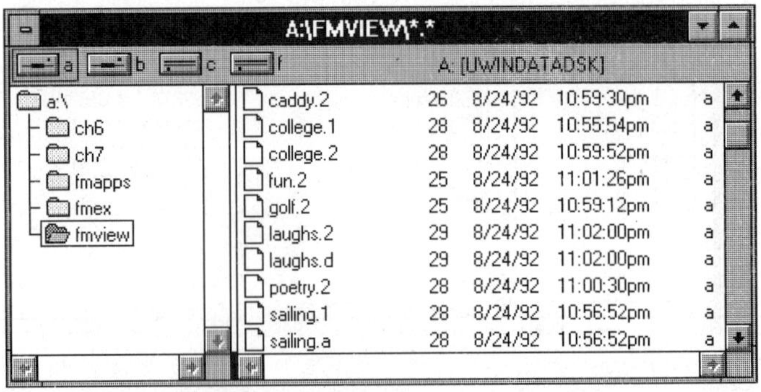

Figure 4.3 The contents of the FMVIEW directory on the Data Disk.

4 In the *directory contents section, double-click* on the icon for the FMVIEW directory and note that your window now appears similar to Figure 4.3.

NOTE: When working in the **directory tree** section, a single click on a directory changes the **directory contents** section to display the items in the chosen directory. When working in the directory contents section, a single click selects an entry; double-clicking on an entry activates it.

5 In the directory contents section, use the scroll bar (if needed) to display the upward pointing arrow (at the top of the directory contents), then double-click on the arrow. The resulting window displays the content of the root directory (and is the same window displayed in step 1).

NOTE: Double-clicking on the upward arrow returns you to the **parent directory** of the directory you were in. In this case the root directory (A:\) is the parent directory to the FMVIEW directory. To complete the relationship, the FMVIEW directory is considered a **child directory** to the root directory. While a parent directory may have many child directories, a child directory has only one parent directory.

Because we are starting to work with a variety of icons, review Figure 4.4 to see an illustration and short explanation of the icons most commonly used to represent files and directories in the directory windows.

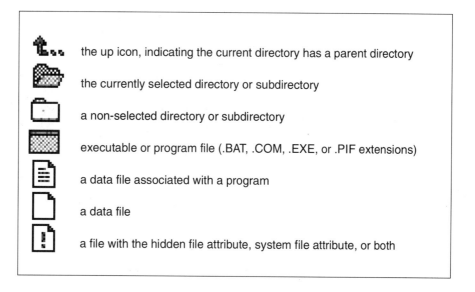

Figure 4.4 Common directory window icons.

Working with the Directory Tree

The first time you use File Manager, the directory tree section shows two levels of detail—the **root directory** and the first level of **subdirectories** under the root. Double-clicking on a directory listing displays its subdirectories (i.e., the parent directory-child directory relationship). Double-clicking on a directory currently displaying its subdirectories hides its subdirectories.

The TREE drop-down menu commands, located in the File Manager window, also provide options for managing the level of detail displayed in the directory tree. Complete the following exercise to practice using the TREE drop-down menu commands.

1. Make sure the directory window displays the items in the root directory of the Data Disk.

2. Click once on the FMEX directory icon in the directory tree. This causes a directory window, similar to Figure 4.5, to be displayed on your desktop.

3. Choose the TREE-Expand One Level command to display the four FMEX subdirectories in the directory tree.

4. Choose the TREE-Collapse Branch to hide the FMEX subdirectories in the directory tree.

5. Move to the directory contents section and double-click on the icon for the JEFF directory. When looking at the directory tree, you see that the FMEX subdirectories are now displayed and the JEFF directory icon appears as an *open* file folder. The STAFF.1, STAFF.2, and STAFF.3 files appear in the contents section.

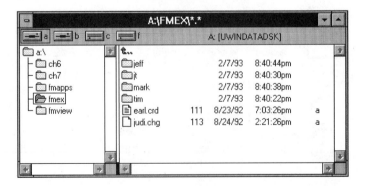

Figure 4.5 The directory window for the FMEX directory.

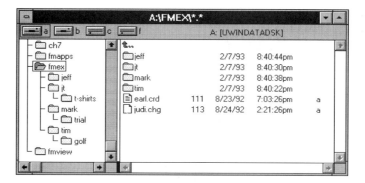

Figure 4.6   The expanded branch view of the FMEX directory.

6   Choose the TREE-Collapse Branch command to *try to* hide the FMEX subdirectories. You will find that you cannot hide a directory's subdirectories when File Manager is using one of those subdirectories as the active directory.

7   Double-click on the FMEX icon, in the directory tree, to make it the current directory and to hide the FMEX subdirectories.

8   Double-click on the JT directory icon (in the directory contents section) to display its contents of a T-SHIRTS subdirectory and three files (SALE.1, SALE.2, and SALE.3). Also, note that the JT file folder now is open in the directory tree.

9   Double-click on the T-SHIRTS directory icon (in the contents section) to display the three PATTERN files. Note that the T-SHIRTS subdirectory is also displayed in the directory tree.

10   Click once on the FMEX icon in the directory tree. Then choose the TREE-Expand Branch command to see the subdirectories under the JT, MARK, and TIM directories. (Your directory window should look similar to Figure 4.6.)

11   Use the scroll bars, if necessary, to display the name of the root directory in the directory tree. Select the root directory, then choose the TREE-Collapse Branch command to hide all the Data Disk subdirectories.

12   Choose the TREE-Expand One Level command to display the five subdirectories of the root. (Your window should be similar to one displayed when you started the exercise.)

TIP: The **directory tree** displays directories at the same level in alphabetical order. To quickly move among directories when the directory tree is active, press the first character of the desired directory name to select the first directory beginning with the character that was pressed. If numerous directories begin with the same character, press the character until the desired directory is selected.

Working with the Directory Contents

When both files and directories are listed in the directory contents, the directories are grouped together (the default setting is in alphabetical order) and placed at the top of the directory contents section. The files are also grouped (in a similar manner to the directories), and listed after the directories. You may customize the file and directory information shown in the directory contents by using the commands from the File Manager VIEW menu.

The purposes of the VIEW menu commands are explained below.

Command	Function
Tree and Directory	Allows for viewing both the tree and contents sections of the directory window.
Tree Only	Displays only the directory tree in the directory window.
Directory Only	Displays only the directory contents in the window.
Split	Activates the split bar to resize the tree and the contents sections.

The following commands affect the appearance of the items in the directory contents.

Name	Displays only the name and extension of each item.
All File Details	Displays all available information regarding the directories and files in the active directory window.
Partial Details	Leads to a dialog box giving the user the option of choosing which item details to display in the directory contents section.
Sort by Name	Lists the directories in alphabetical order followed by an alphabetized list of files.
Sort by Type	Lists the directories in alphabetical order followed by the files listed in alphabetical order by extension.
Sort by Size	Lists the directories in alphabetical order followed by the files listed by byte size (largest to smallest).

Each of the commands, except the "Split" and "By File Type... " commands, is an option that can be activated or deactivated. When a command (excluding "Split" and "By File Type...") has been activated, a check mark is placed in front of the choice on the VIEW drop-down menu.

Complete the following exercise to practice using the VIEW menu.

1 Display the root directory of your Data Disk.

2 If necessary, move the split bar so that the directory contents section covers two-thirds of the width of the directory window width. Then select the FMVIEW directory.

3 If not already chosen, choose the VIEW-All File Details command to display all the details for the entries in the directory contents.

4 Choose the VIEW-Partial Details... command to display the Partial Details dialog box (see Figure 4.7).

In Figure 4.7, all check boxes are marked with an "X" indicating that all file details will be displayed. Clicking on a check box turns it on or off. When the option is turned off, the box is empty.

5 To change the appearance of the directory contents so that only the item name, extension, and byte size are displayed, clear all the check boxes except the size check box. Then choose OK.

Your directory window should now list only the item names, extensions, and byte sizes listed in the directory contents.

6 Choose the VIEW-All File Details to redisplay all the information for each entry.

7 Choose the VIEW-Sort by Type command to group the files alphabetically by extensions (in this case, you see that extensions starting with numbers—smallest to largest—are listed before extensions starting with letters), and then by filename. Use the scroll bar to verify that the files are in the proper order.

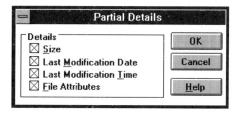

Figure 4.7 The Partial Details dialog box.

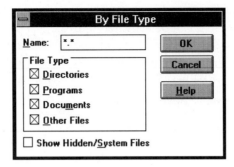

Figure 4.8 The By File Type dialog box.

8 Choose the VIEW-Sort by Name command to display the filenames in alphabetical order.

9 Choose the VIEW-Sort by Size command to arrange each file by its byte size, listing largest to smallest.

10 Choose the VIEW-Sort by Date command to arrange each file by its last modification date, starting with the most recent date.

11 Choose the VIEW-By File Type... command to display the By File Type dialog box (see Figure 4.8).

Enter **C*.*** in the text box, to instruct File Manager to display only the filenames beginning with the letter "C" in the directory contents. (The * following the letter "C" represents all remaining characters in the name of any file beginning with the letter "C." The * following the period represents any extension.)

Choose the OK button. Your directory window should display only the files beginning with the letter "C" (these files consist of college.2, caddy.2, and college.1).

12 Display all the files in the FMVIEW directory. (Hint: Enter *.* in the Name text box of the By File Type dialog box.)

Working with Disks

The File Manager DISK drop-down menu commands enable you to: format, copy, and create labels for disks; create system disks; and change drives. (When running Windows on a network, the DISK menu may also include commands for connecting or disconnecting your computer from a network and for connecting to/disconnecting from a network drive. Please refer to File Manager Help for further information regarding these network commands.)

Formatting Floppy Disks

When you format a disk, you prepare it to store information. You may format a blank disk, or a disk that already has information stored on it. The formatting process removes all previous information from the disk, creates new storage information, and marks any bad (unusable) segments of the disk.

In the following exercise you will use File Manager to format a disk. (The disk may be blank or may hold files you no longer need.) **DO NOT FORMAT YOUR DATA DISK,** as it is needed for the remaining chapters.

1   Insert either a blank disk, or a disk holding files you no longer need, into the desired drive and choose the DISK-Format Disk... command. This command displays the Format Disk dialog box. (See Figure 4.9.)

2   If the appropriate drive is not displayed in the Disk In drop-down list box, click on the down arrow button to display the list of drives, and then select the appropriate drive.

3   Use the Capacity drop-down list box, in the same manner you did in step 2, to select the capacity corresponding to your disk.

Figure 4.9   The Format Disk dialog box.

NOTE: The easiest way to determine a disk's capacity is to look at its label (or the box it came in). A **double-density** (or low density) disk is normally marked **DD;** a **high density** disk is normally marked **HD.** If the disk has no labeling, check for the physical characteristics listed below:

Disk	Storage Capacity	Physical Characteristics
5.25-inch DD	360K (kilobytes)	hub ring around center hole
5.25-inch HD	1.2 MB (megabytes)	no hub ring
3.5-inch DD	720K	small square hole in one corner
3.5-inch HD	1.44 MB	small square hole in two corners

4   Select the Label text box in the Options section, and enter UWINDATA2 as the label for the disk being formatted. (If you want to change the label on a disk, without reformatting the disk, use the DISK-Label Disk... command.)

Although we will not use either of the remaining choices in the Options section, you may want to use them at a later time.

TIP:

1. The Make a System Disk option copies the MS-DOS system files onto the disk being formatted. This disk can then be used to start (or boot) a computer using the MS-DOS operating system.

2. The Quick Format option may be used only with a previously formatted disk. When the option is selected, the disk's root directory and file allocation table are deleted; however, the disk is not scanned for bad sectors. Because the scanning process is omitted, this option speeds the formatting process.

5   Choose OK.

6   A confirmation dialog box appears warning that formatting a disk removes all information on the disk. Choose Yes to initiate the format command. Watch the Formatting Disk dialog box to monitor the formatting process.

7   After the formatting is completed, another dialog box appears asking if you want to format another disk. Choose No.

NOTE: When the directory window is displaying the contents of a floppy disk and you *change* disks, the contents are *not* automatically updated. To update the window after changing disks, choose the WINDOW-Refresh command or press F5.

8   Press F5 (or choose the WINDOW-Refresh command) to display the contents of the newly formatted disk. The volume label should appear in the disk drive icon bar; however, no files are displayed because no program or document files have been placed on the disk.

NOTE: If you place an unformatted disk in a drive and then try to open a directory window for that disk, the Error Selecting Drive dialog box will appear stating that the disk is not formatted. By choosing Yes in that dialog box, you will start the formatting procedure.

Making a Copy of a Disk

To make an exact copy of a disk, the **source** (original) disk and the **destination** (target) disk must have the same capacities. This command is similar to the MS-DOS diskcopy command. If the disk you formatted in the previous exercise has the same dimensions and storage capacity as your Data Disk, complete the following exercise to practice making a copy of a disk. In the steps below, we will use the same drive for the source and destination disks. If your computer system has two identical disk drives, follow the directions in the dialog boxes to take advantage of using both drives at the same time.

1. Insert your original Data Disk (the source disk) into the drive you plan to copy from. Refresh the window to display the contents of the disk. (If you have two identical drives, place the destination disk into the drive you plan to copy to.)

2. Choose the DISK-Copy Disk... command.

   For computers having two or more floppy drives, a Copy Disk dialog box appears (see Figure 4.10) instructing you to choose the source and destination drives. This dialog box is not displayed if the computer has only one floppy drive.

   In Figure 4.10, drive A serves as both the source and destination drive. Choose the proper drives to meet your copying situation.

   After selecting the drives, choose OK.

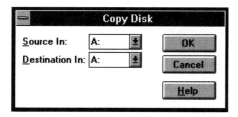

Figure 4.10 The Copy Disk dialog box.

3 A confirmation box appears on your desktop asking you to verify that you plan to copy onto the destination disk. (This type of copying procedure removes any previously saved files on the destination disk.) Choose Yes to continue the copying procedure.

4 If you are using only one drive, follow the on-screen directions for inserting the source disk and then replacing the source disk with the destination disk. During the copying procedure, the Copying Disk dialog box provides a **percentage completed indicator** to show how much of the procedure has been accomplished. When the copying process is finished the Copy Disk dialog box automatically closes.

5 After the copying procedure is finished, verify that the copy was made by refreshing the directory window corresponding to the drive holding your destination disk.

Quitting File Manager

As with other Windows programs, there are numerous ways to quit File Manager. Most users tend either to use the FILE-Exit command or to double-click on the Control-menu box. If you choose to make File Manager your Windows default shell, when you exit File Manager you exit Windows and return to the DOS prompt.

Summary

File Manager, the application used to manipulate your files and directories, is one of the most important programs in Windows. Because of its features and increased speed, the Windows 3.1 version of File Manager is a major improvement over the Windows 3.0 version.

Along with the standard elements found in application windows (window borders, title bar, Control-menu box, sizing buttons, menu bar, and work area), the File Manager window also includes a status bar. The **status bar** is located along the bottom of the window and displays information such as bytes free, total bytes used, and the number of files on the current disk.

The File Manager document windows are referred to as **directory windows.** Directory windows consist of the standard document window elements (window borders, title bar, Control-menu box, and sizing buttons) and three unique window sections. The first section, the **disk drive icon bar** located under the title bar, displays icons representing the drives you may access through File Manager. The second section, the **directory tree** located on the left side of the document window, displays the directory (and subdirectory) structure of the current disk. The third section, the **directory contents** located on the right side of the window, displays the contents of the selected directory in the directory tree. A **vertical split bar** (which may be moved left or right) separates the directory tree and directory contents sections and determines the width of each section.

Selection cursors are used to indicate which items have been selected. A selection cursor may be found in each of the three sections of the directory window, although only one selection cursor may be active at one time. **Inactive cursors** form a rectangle around the selected item. An **active selection cursor** surrounds the item and displays it in reverse video.

The simplest way to **change the directory contents** is to click on a different directory in the directory tree. If a directory is listed in the directory contents section, you may double-click on it to display its items in the directory window.

File Manager drop-down menu commands discussed in this chapter included:

1. **TREE commands,** which control the levels of directories displayed in the directory tree.

2. **VIEW commands,** which control the appearance of the directory window, the amount of DOS information listed next to the name of each file and directory, and the order of appearance for the files and directories in the directory window.

3. **DISK commands,** which enable you to format and copy disks, create disk labels, and create system disks.

Applications

Use the directories and files located on your Data Disk to complete the following applications:

Application 1

1. Open a directory window for the FMAPPS directory on your Data Disk. The five icons and titles for the ANNIE, GREG, JENNY, JOSH, and KIRSTEN subdirectories should appear in the directory contents section.

2. Complete the following steps to manipulate the appearance of the directory window:

   a. Drag the vertical split bar until the directory contents section fills two-thirds of the directory window width.

   b. Click on the root directory in the directory tree. Use one command from the TREE menu to display all branches of all directories in the directory tree section. Then use one command from the TREE menu to display only the root directory in the directory tree section.

   c. Expand the directory tree to display one level of directories under the root directory. Use the VIEW menu to display only the directory contents section in the directory window. Then change the window to display both the directory tree and the directory contents.

   d. Select the FMAPPS directory in the directory tree. Open the GREG directory to display its three files. Show only the corresponding DOS statistics of byte size and time of last modification. Arrange the files in the directory by size.

   e. Select the proper VIEW menu commands to display all the file details and to list the directories and files in alphabetical order.

Application 2

1. Open a directory window for the FMVIEW directory on your Data Disk. Working with the proper VIEW menu command and dialog box, display only the files within the FMVIEW directory window having a .1 extension.

2. Keeping the File Manager window open, open the Notepad accessory (which you used in the previous end-of-chapter applications) and enter your name on the first line. Enter "Chapter 4 - Application 2" on the second line and press Enter twice. Then make a list of the filenames you displayed in step 1. (You should find seven files. List two files per line, except for the last line, in your Notepad document.) Print this list using the Notepad default printer settings.

3. Close the Notepad accessory without saving the file.

4. Modify the procedure you used in step 1, so that all of the files in the FMVIEW directory are displayed in the directory contents section. (Make sure to complete this step before starting Application 3.)

Application 3

1. Open the Notepad accessory and enter your name on the first line. Enter "Chapter 4 - Application 3" on the second line and press Enter twice. Then create the following two table headings FILE and DIRECTORY. (Separate FILE and DIRECTORY by pressing Tab twice.) List the following files under the FILE heading (one file per line): Sale.1, Trial.3, Student.2, Card.1, Pattern.2, and Case.1.

2. Keeping the Notepad window open, open a File Manager directory window for the FMEX directory. Each of the files listed in step 1 is located in a different subdirectory of the FMEX directory. Find the various directories containing the files listed in step 1, and list the corresponding directory across from the filename in your Notepad document.

3. After recording the corresponding directories to the files, print your Notepad document (using the default settings).

4. Close the Notepad accessory without saving the file.

5

File Manager—Part II

In the previous chapter you learned to work with the File Manager directory windows to display the contents of various directories on your Data Disk. You also used the File Manager menu bar to control the appearance of the windows and conduct various disk operations.

File Manager is most commonly used to manipulate files and directories. In this chapter you will learn to use File Manager to move, copy, delete, rename, associate, and print files. You will also learn the File Manager procedures for creating, moving, copying, renaming, and deleting directories.

Creating Directories

The basic reason for creating a directory is to store related files in a common location.

In the following exercises you will find that using File Manager makes it easy to create directories and manipulate their contents.

1 Start Windows and open the File Manager window.

2 Place your Data Disk in the appropriate drive, then open a directory window displaying the contents of your Data Disk.

3 Before creating a new directory, you must select the parent directory for the directory you are about to create. Click once on the FMEX directory to make it the active directory.

4 Choose the FILE-Create Directory... command to display the Create Directory dialog box (see Figure 5.1).

5 In the Name text box, key the name PATTY.1 for the name of the first new directory.

6 Choose the OK button to create a directory named PATTY.1 on the same level as the JEFF, JT, MARK, and TIM directories.

7 Repeat the necessary steps above to create another directory named PATTY.2 on the same level as the PATTY.1 directory. When you complete this step, your directory window should look similar to the one in Figure 5.2.

Create Directory	
Current Directory: A:\FMEX	OK
Name:	Cancel
	Help

Figure 5.1 The Create Directory dialog box.

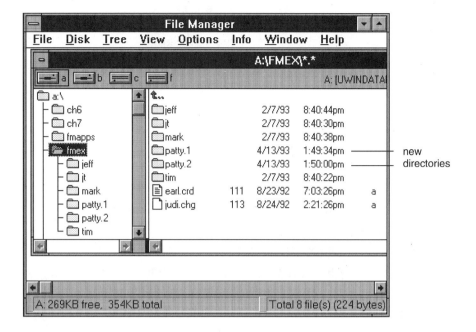

Figure 5.2   Results of steps 1–7.

Manipulating Files and Directories

Manipulating files and directories is a two-step process. The first step is to select the desired items (files and/or directories). The second step is to execute the commands to move, copy, rename, delete, associate, or print the selected items.

Selecting Items

The following section describes how to use the mouse to select items in the *directory contents section* of a directory window.

To select a single file or directory:

1. Click on the icon (or name) of the desired file or directory.

NOTE: To deselect an item, click on any file or directory in the directory window.

To select a consecutive group of items:

1. Click on the first item of the group

2. Depress the Shift key then click on the last item in the group. This will cause the first, last, and all items between the two to appear highlighted.

NOTE:

1. To deselect a group of items, click on any file or directory in the directory window.

2. To deselect an item within a group of selected items, place the pointer on the item to be deselected, depress the Ctrl key and click the mouse.

3. To select two or more groups of consecutive items in the same directory window:

    a. Select the first group using the Shift key procedure discussed above.

    b. Move the pointer to the first item in the second group, depress the Ctrl key, then click the mouse's button once.

    c. Move the pointer to the last item in the group, depress the Shift and Ctrl key and click the mouse button once.

TIP: | A fast way to select all the items in a directory is to make the directory contents section active and then press Ctrl+Slash(/).

To select a nonconsecutive group of items:

1. Click on the first item.

2. Hold down the Ctrl key while clicking on the rest of the items in the desired group.

A convenient way to select a large group of files, having a common characteristic in the filename or extension, is to use the Select Files... command in the FILE menu. This command also provides a quick method to select a few related files from a directory holding many files. By using this command, you do not need to scan through the entire directory contents to find the files before you select them. Choosing this command displays the Select Files dialog box (see Figure 5.3).

To use this command, complete the steps below:

1. Choose the FILE-Select Files... command to display the Select Files dialog box.

2. Choose the Deselect button to clear any previously selected items. (This action also causes the Cancel button to change to a Close button.) Then

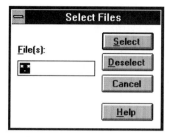

Figure 5.3 The Select Files dialog box.

check the File Manager Window Status Bar to see that 0 items have been selected.

3. In the text box, key the common characteristic of a group of files to be selected, along with the appropriate DOS wildcards (such as *.DOC).

4. Choose the Select button to select the items and then choose Close.

Moving and Copying Files and Directories

Moving an item erases it from its current location and places it in a new location. **Copying** an item leaves the original item in place and inserts a duplicate item in a new location. The ease in moving and copying files and directories is one of the greatest benefits of Windows. The key to this easy moving and copying is the **drag-and-drop** feature of File Manager. When you use this feature you simply drag the icon representing the selected item(s) onto another directory window, directory icon, or drive icon and then release the mouse button. (Items placed on a drive icon will be inserted into the drive's current directory.) When moving or copying items, the **source** is the original location and the **destination** is the new location.

As you will soon see, the move and copy commands are very similar. It is easy to get the commands confused, so Windows provides a quick way to let you see if you are copying or moving items. When the icon being moved from the source reaches its destination, *before* releasing the mouse button, see if the icon displays a plus sign (+). A "+" appearing in the icon indicates that the selected item(s) will be *copied* into the new location. If the icon remains blank upon reaching its destination, the items will be *moved* into the new location.

Complete the following exercise to learn the various File Manager moving and copying techniques. (This exercise also shows you how to display two, or more, directory windows at the same time.) All moving and copying procedures occur on your Data Disk. To keep your Windows environment intact, DO NOT move any of the original Windows files from their current location.

1 Open a directory window displaying the contents of the FMEX directory. (For ease in viewing, maximize the File Manager window.) Expand the FMEX branch to show all of its subdirectories. (Hint: Use the TREE-Expand Branch command.)

Change the directory contents by selecting the GOLF subdirectory, underneath the TIM directory, in the directory tree.

2 Use the VIEW-Partial Details... command to remove all the file details from the directory contents section. This results in only the file/directory names and extensions appearing in the directory contents section.

3 Open a second directory window to display the JEFF directory by completing the following steps:

a. Choose the WINDOW-New Window command. (This results in a duplicate A:\FMEX\TIM\GOLF*.* window appearing on your desktop. Note that the title of the original window ends with a :1, while :2 is attached to the title of the second window.)

b. In the second window, click on the JEFF directory (in the directory tree) to display its contents.

4 Open the WINDOW menu, depress the Shift key and choose the WINDOW-Tile command to organize your directory windows to appear similar to those in Figure 5.4.

5 Move the CARD.1 file from the GOLF directory to the JEFF directory by:

a. Selecting the CARD.1 file in the GOLF directory window.

b. Dragging the icon representing the selected file into the directory contents section of the JEFF directory window. (Note that there is no "+" within the icon being moved.)

c. Releasing the mouse button to display the Confirm Mouse Operation dialog box. Choose Yes to initiate the action and note the briefly appearing Moving... dialog box on the desktop while the move is occurring.

6 Copy the CARD.2 and CARD.3 files from the GOLF directory into the JEFF directory by:

a. Selecting the two files as a consecutive group in the GOLF window (and keep the mouse button depressed and move to step 6).

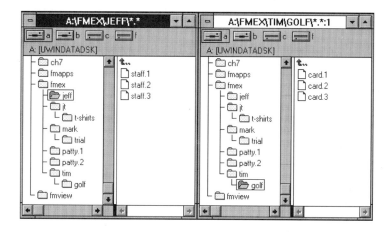

Figure 5.4 The FMEX\JEFF and FMEX\TIM\GOLF directory windows.

b. Depressing the Ctrl key and dragging the selected files icon on top of the JEFF directory icon in the GOLF window. (Notice the icon being dragged contains a "+" to indicate that a copy procedure is occurring.)

c. Releasing the mouse button, and then releasing the Ctrl key to display the Confirm Mouse Operation dialog box. Choose Yes to initiate the action and note the briefly appearing Copying... dialog box on the desktop while the copy procedure is occurring. Your window should now appear similar to Figure 5.5.

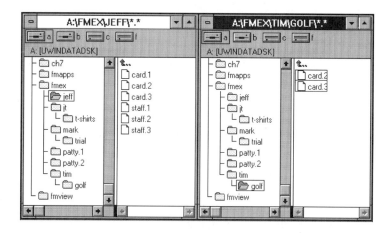

Figure 5.5 The directory windows after completing step 6.

NOTE: Although it is not necessary to open a destination directory window when conducting a moving or copying procedure, this does allow you to immediately view the results of your actions.

7   Close the JEFF directory window. Maximize the GOLF directory window inside the File Manager window. (Notice the change in the File Manager title bar.)

8   Change the directory contents by selecting the T-SHIRTS subdirectory of the JT directory.

9   *Move* the file PATTERN.1 to the PATTY.1 directory without opening a directory window for the PATTY.1 directory.

10   Open a new directory window for PATTY.1 to observe the results of step 9.

11   While working only in the directory tree section, *move* the T-SHIRTS directory from the JT directory into the PATTY.1 directory by:

a. Selecting the T-SHIRTS directory.

b. Dragging the icon on top of the PATTY.1 directory.

c. Releasing the mouse button. Choose Yes in the Confirm Mouse Operation dialog box. This step will move the directory and its files. (If the move is successful, the T-SHIRTS directory is now under the PATTY.1 directory.)

12   While working only in the directory tree section, *copy* the TRIAL directory from the MARK directory into the PATTY.2 directory by:

a. Selecting the TRIAL directory and keeping the mouse button depressed.

b. Depressing the Ctrl key and dragging the icon on top of the PATTY.2 directory.

c. Releasing the mouse button, and then the Ctrl key to display the Confirm Mouse Operation dialog box. Choose Yes to confirm the copying of the TRIAL directory and its files. Your directory tree should now resemble the one in Figure 5.6.

Deleting Files and Directories

Removing unnecessary files and directories from your disks is an important part of keeping your computing environment organized. (This also saves storage space on your disks.) File Manager makes it easy to remove files and directories. Just select what you want to delete and either press the Delete key or choose the FILE-Delete... command.

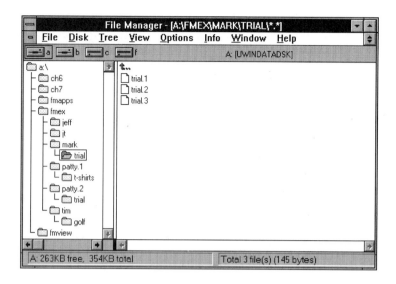

Figure 5.6 The File Manager window after completing step 12.

In the exercise below, you will work with your Data Disk to remove some of the files and directories used in the previous exercise.

1 If necessary, adjust your desktop to look similar to Figure 5.6.

2 Selecting the JEFF directory in the directory tree.

3 Delete the CARD.2 file by selecting it and then choosing the FILE-Delete... command (or pressing Delete).

When the Delete dialog box appears, choose OK.

When the Confirm File Delete dialog box appears, choose Yes. This action deletes the CARD.2 file.

Repeat these steps to delete the CARD.3 file.

The JEFF directory should now contain the CARD.1, STAFF.1, STAFF.2, and STAFF.3 files.

TIP: In the step above, selecting the CARD.2 and CARD.3 files as a group, choosing FILE-Delete and then choosing the Yes to All button, instead of the Yes button in the Confirm File Delete dialog box, would have deleted the CARD.2 and the CARD.3 files at the same time.

NOTE: Windows allows a directory containing files to be removed from the disk. In the following steps you will remove the TRIAL subdirectory (and its files) from under the PATTY.2 directory.

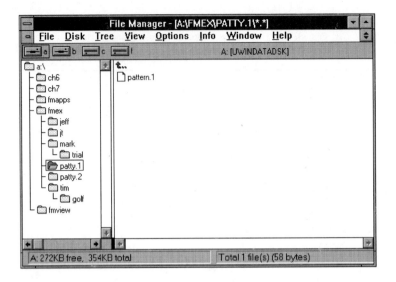

Figure 5.7 The directory tree of the Data Disk after completing step 7.

4 Select the TRIAL subdirectory under the PATTY.2 directory in the directory tree.

5 Choose the FILE-Delete... command to display the Delete dialog box.

6 Choose OK to display the Confirm Directory Delete dialog box. Choose Yes to confirm the deletion. Choose Yes to All in the Confirm File Delete dialog box to delete all the TRIAL files.

NOTE: When you delete a directory containing files, the Confirm File Delete dialog box appears to give you one last chance to save the files from deletion.

7 Using the information from the previous steps, delete the T-SHIRTS directory underneath the PATTY.1 directory. When you finish this step, your directory tree should be similar to the one in Figure 5.7.

Renaming Files or Directories

Sometimes it's necessary to rename a file or directory. Complete the following exercise to learn the procedure to rename a file or directory.

1 Select the FMEX directory in the directory tree.

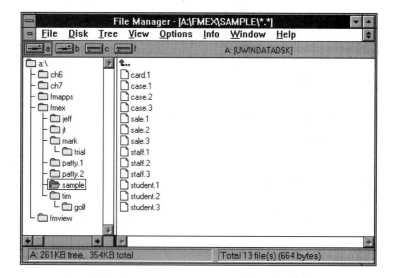

Figure 5.8 The directory window after completing step 3.

2 Use the FILE-Create Directory... command to create a directory, named SAMPLE, under the FMEX directory. Then, if it is not already selected, choose the VIEW-Sort by Name command.

3 Copy only the *files* from the JEFF, JT, MARK, and TIM directories into the SAMPLE directory. Upon completing this step, select the SAMPLE directory, in the directory tree. Your directory window should be similar to Figure 5.8.

4 Rename the STUDENT.1 file to PUPIL.1 using the following steps:

a. Select the STUDENT.1 file in the directory contents section.

b. Choose the FILE-Rename... command to display the Rename dialog box (see Figure 5.9).

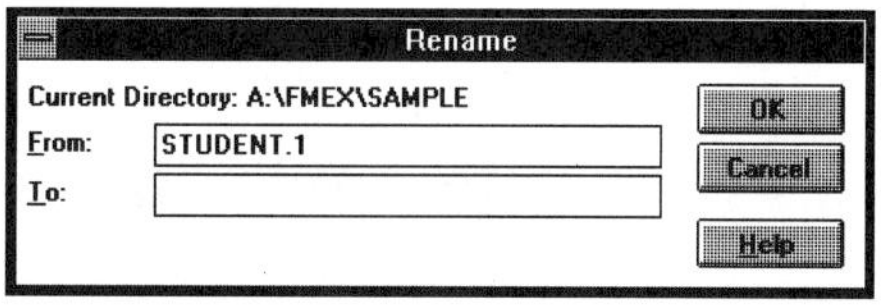

Figure 5.9 The Rename dialog box.

    c. The selected file or directory name is already placed in the From text box. Enter the new name in the To text box.

    For this exercise enter PUPIL.1 in the To text box.

    d. Choose OK (or press Enter) to complete the rename procedure and then check your results in the directory contents.

5   Rename two additional files in the SAMPLE directory.

6   Repeat the above procedure to rename the directory from SAMPLE to PRACTICE. (Hint: Your first step is to select the SAMPLE directory from the directory tree.)

Starting Applications from File Manager

Although File Manager's primary purpose is to help you manage your files, directories, and disks, you may also start applications from File Manager. To start an application from the File Manager window, choose the FILE-Run... command. Then enter the name of the program's executable file in the Run dialog box. (Most executable files have a .COM, .EXE, .PIF, or .BAT extension.) This command procedure is also available under the Program Manager FILE menu.

    Complete the following exercise to launch the Calculator and Clock accessories through the use of File Manager's FILE-Run... command. (If your Windows package has been installed in the standard manner, the path command in your AUTOEXEC.BAT file enables you to start the Calculator and Clock accessories, even though the directory path in the Run dialog box refers to the location of your Data Disk.)

1   Choose the FILE-Run... command from the File Manager menu bar.

2   When the Run dialog box appears, enter CALC.EXE in the text box and press Enter to launch the Calculator.

3   Close the Calculator and repeat steps 1 and 2 using the CLOCK.EXE file to launch the Clock accessory.

4   Close the Clock window.

Associating Document Files with Applications

The File Manager FILE-Associate... command is used to **associate** a document file with an application. Once a document file has been associated with an application, the application can be launched by double-clicking on the document's name (or icon) in a directory window.

A file that is associated with an application is displayed with an icon that looks like a dog-eared sheet of paper containing horizontal lines. A file that is not associated with an application is displayed with an icon that looks like a blank dog-eared sheet of paper.

In the following exercise you will learn how to launch an application through the use of an associated file in a directory window.

1 Open a directory window for the FMEX directory on your Data Disk.

2 Note that the EARL.CRD file icon contains horizontal lines, indicating that the file is associated with an application (in this case, the Windows Cardfile).

3 Note that the JUDI.CHG file icon is blank, indicating that the file is not associated with an application.

4 Double-click on the EARL.CRD file icon to launch the Cardfile application and load the EARL.CRD file. (The file contains the address for Lillie Earl.)

5 Close the Cardfile by double-clicking on the (Cardfile) Control-menu box.

6 Double-click on the JUDI.CHG file icon to view the Cannot Run Program dialog box, which states that the file is not associated with an application.

7 Choose OK to close the dialog box.

Windows uses the filename **extension** to associate files with applications. When applications are set up through Windows, all corresponding associations are recorded in a table referred to as the registration database. When Windows is set up, associations for Cardfile, Paintbrush, Write, Terminal, Calendar, Recorder, and Notepad—the Windows accessories that allow for saving files—are automatically created and recorded.

Not all files are immediately associated with an application. Complete the exercise below to learn the steps for associating a file with an application.

1 Open a directory window for the FMEX directory on your Data Disk. (It may still be open from the previous exercise.)

2 Select the JUDI.CHG file (a nonassociated file), then choose the FILE-Associate... command to display the Associate dialog box (see Figure 5.10).

The entry in the Files with Extension text box should read CHG. (If it does not, enter CHG in this text box before moving to the next step.)

3 Move to the Associate With list box and select "Card File (cardfile.exe)." This causes the words "Card File" to be displayed in the Associate With text box.

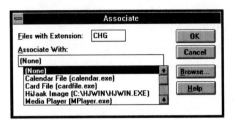

Figure 5.10   The Associate dialog box.

Then choose the OK button to associate all files with a CHG extension with the Cardfile accessory.

4   Note the changed appearance of the icon next to the JUDI.CHG file name. (Horizontal lines now appear on the dog-eared sheet.) Double-click on the icon to launch the Cardfile accessory and load the JUDI.CHG file. (The file contains the address of a person named Judi Carol.)

5   Close the Cardfile accessory by double-clicking on the Control-menu box.

TIP: Many Windows users associate files that are frequently used (i.e., daily spreadsheet files) with their corresponding applications. This procedure, of using one command to launch the application and load the associated file, is more efficient than the traditional routine of loading an application, opening the desired directory to find the document file, and then loading the appropriate file.

There may be times when it is necessary to remove an association. Complete the following exercise to remove the association between the CHG extension and the Cardfile application.

1   Select the JUDI.CHG file.

2   Choose the FILE-Associate... command. Note that CHG has been entered in the Files with Extension text box.

3   Select the (None) option in the Associate With list.

4   Choose OK to complete the action.

5   Note the changed appearance of the icon with the JUDI.CHG file.

6 Double-click on the JUDI.CHG file to view the dialog box stating that the file is not associated with an application.

7 Choose OK to close the Cannot Run Program dialog box.

Printing a File

If files are associated with applications, they may usually be printed directly from File Manager (without first separately launching the application that was used to create them). Two ways to initiate the printing of associated files are:

1. Select the file(s), choose the FILE-Print... command, then choose OK in the Print dialog box.

2. If the Print Manager has been opened from the Program Manager Main window and is displayed as either an open window or a minimized window icon, drag the selected document icon from a directory window to the Print Manager window or minimized icon.

Either choice will cause the associated program to open. Windows will then use the program's normal printing procedure to print the document(s).

Searching for Files or Directories

Because users generally work with large numbers of files and directories, occasionally a person may forget where a particular file or directory is located. In the following exercise, you will learn to use the FILE-Search... command, which enables File Manager to quickly search your disks and directories to identify the location of misplaced item(s). In this exercise, you will start your search from the root directory of the Data Disk and locate all of the files on the disk that begin with the letter "s."

1 Usually, the first step in the Search procedure is to select the directory from which to start your search. For this exercise, select the root directory (A:\) of your Data Disk.

Figure 5.11 The Search dialog box.

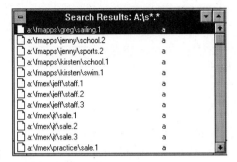

Figure 5.12 The Search Results window.

2 Choose the FILE-Search... command to display the Search dialog box.

3 Enter the name of the item you are searching for in the Search For text box. For this exercise, enter s*.* (to search for all files beginning with an "s"). The information in the Start From text box corresponds with the directory you selected in Step 1. For this problem, make sure the Search All Subdirectories option is selected. (After you enter this data, the dialog box should look like the one in Figure 5.11.)

4 Choose the OK button to start the search.

5 View the results of the search. Your Search Results window should be similar to the one in Figure 5.12.

NOTE: Once the missing files or directories are displayed in the Search Results window, they can be selected and printed, moved, copied, deleted, associated, or renamed (just as any other item in a directory window). You may not, however, move or copy items *into* the Search Results window.

6 Repeat the above steps to search for all the files on your Data Disk that begin with the letter "e". Entering a new search criterion will automatically clear the previous Search Results window. (Hint: Your Search Results window should display only the EARL.CRD file.)

7 Close the Search Results window.

Saving the Settings

Upon exiting File Manager, to save the positions of the directory windows and icons, along with any changes made through the VIEW menu, make sure a check mark appears next to the OPTIONS-Save Settings on Exit command. This option may be turned on or off by opening the OPTIONS menu and clicking on the Save Settings on Exit command.

TIP: When working with either File Manager or Program Manager, if you have created an arrangement you really like, you may save the settings without exiting the program by depressing the Shift key and choosing the FILE-Exit command from the File Manager menu bar.

Summary

This chapter focused on manipulating files and directories through the File Manager menu commands and mouse operations. Some of the chapter topics included: selecting, moving, copying, deleting, renaming, and printing items; associating files with applications; and searching for items.

Use the **FILE-Create Directory... command** to create a directory underneath the selected directory in the directory tree.

To select items in the directory contents:

1. To select one item, click on it with the mouse.

2. To select a consecutive group of items, click on the first item, scroll to the last item of the group, depress the Shift key and click on the last item.

3. To select a nonconsecutive group of items, depress the Ctrl key and then click on the desired items.

4. The FILE-Select Files... command is most appropriate to use when all the files to be selected have a common characteristic (i.e., the same extension).

Moving and copying steps:

1. *To move items within the same drive,* drag the selected items icon from the source to the destination and release the mouse button.

2. *To move items to a different drive,* select the items, keeping the mouse button depressed after selecting the last item. Then hold down the Shift key while dragging the selected items icon to the desired location. Release the mouse button, and then release the Shift key.

3. *To copy items within the same drive,* select the items, keeping the mouse button depressed after selecting the last item. Then hold down the Ctrl key while dragging the selected items icon to the desired location. Release the mouse button, and then release the Ctrl key.

4. *To copy items to a different drive,* drag the selected items icon to the new destination and release the mouse button. (Holding down the Control key during this procedure is not required.)

5. Moving/copying entire directories on the same disk can be accomplished by working within the directory tree.

Renaming and deleting items are simple processes carried out through the FILE menu and the corresponding dialog boxes.

Windows uses the filename extension to associate files with applications. By default, when Windows is first installed, associations are already set up for the Cardfile, Paintbrush, Write, Terminal, Calendar, Recorder, and Notepad accessories. To create a new association:

1. a. Choose the FILE-Associate... command and enter the name of the desired extension in the Files with Extension text box or,

   b. Select a file that utilizes the extension to be associated and then choose the FILE-Associate... command. The extension will automatically appear in the File with Extension text box.

2. Select the desired application, from the Associate With drop-down list box, to be associated with the extension identified in Step 1.

3. Choose the OK button.

To initiate the printing of an associated file from File Manager:
Either select the desired files and drag the selected icons on top of the Print Manager open window or minimized window icon, or select the files, choose the FILE-Print... command to display the Print dialog box, and then choose OK. The corresponding application will load and the file will be printed through the program's print procedure.

The **FILE-Search... procedure** is used to find misplaced items on your disk. Results of the search are placed in the Search Results window.

Applications

All of the following applications utilize your Data Disk. There is no need to change any of the Windows files to complete the applications.

Application 1

1. Create a directory, named JFILES, within the FMAPPS directory that is at the same level as the ANNIE, GREG, JENNY, JOSH, and KIRSTEN directories.

2. Copy only the *files* from the JOSH directory into the JFILES directory. (The JOSH directory should not appear as a subdirectory of JFILES.)

3. Select the FMAPPS directory. Use the FILE-Search... command to find all the files within all the FMAPPS subdirectories having a .1 extension. In one copy procedure, copy all of the files having a .1 extension into the JFILES directory.

NOTE: When you complete this step a message appears in the Search Results dialog box stating that the contents of the drive have changed and asking if you would like to update the Search Results window. Choose No and close the Search Results window.

4. Select the JFILES directory, in the directory tree, to display the JFILES directory contents. Use the FILE-Select Files... command to select all files within JFILES that start with the letter "C" and have a .2 extension. Then delete the selected files.

5. Locate the file THOUGHTS.2 (somewhere within the FMAPPS subdirectories) and copy the file into JFILES. Do not update the drive contents. Close the Search Results window.

Application 2

1. Create a directory named CH5APP2 within the FMAPPS directory that is at the same level as the ANNIE, GREG, JENNY, and JFILES directories.

2. Open a directory window showing the contents of the JFILES directory and select all the files starting with an "s" or "t." In one move procedure, move all the selected files into the CH5APP2 directory.

3. Copy the GREG directory into your CH5APP2 directory. (The copied GREG directory should appear as a subdirectory to the CH5APP2 directory.)

Application 3

1. Create a directory named CH5APP3 within the FMAPPS directory that is at the same level as the ANNIE, CH5APP2, and JFILES directories.

2. Copy the files in the JENNY directory into the CH5APP3 directory. (The JENNY directory should not appear as a subdirectory of CH5APP3.)

3. Copy the entire *contents* of the CH5APP2 directory (not including the CH5APP2 directory itself) into the CH5APP3 directory.

4. Remove the GREG directory from the CH5APP3 directory.

Application 4

1. Place a copy of the revised FMAPPS directory, from your Data Disk, on the extra disk you formatted when you completed Chapter 4.

6

Desktop Accessories

Windows includes a number of helpful accessory programs that are designed to be used *while* running typical software applications. For example, if you were writing a document using the Word for Windows word processing package, you could also be running the Windows Paintbrush accessory to create some illustrations to add to your document.

This chapter examines five of the most commonly used accessories. The Clock and the Calculator, two of the most straightforward accessories, are discussed first. The Notepad accessory, which is primarily used to create short notes and edit text files, is reviewed next. Included in the Notepad discussion are the procedures for saving files, printing files, and opening previously saved files. Because all Windows applications follow the same basic procedures for saving, printing, and opening files, completing this section also helps you learn some very fundamental Windows file procedures. The Calendar accessory, which is used to set up your daily/monthly calendars will then be discussed. The Cardfile accessory, the Windows notecard organizer, is the last accessory examined in this chapter. The chapter concludes by briefly discussing accessories that require additional hardware to function with your system.

Clock

The purpose of the Clock accessory is to display the current time (date is optional) on your screen. It is the simplest Windows accessory and uses a small amount of memory (approximately 18K). The Clock may be displayed in analog or digital settings (see Figure 6.1).

The menu bar in the Clock window consists of only the SETTINGS drop-down menu. Complete the following exercise to see the effect of the SETTINGS commands on the Clock window.

1 Open the Program Manager window, then open the Accessories window.

2 Double-click on the Clock icon to open the Clock window. If the traditional clock face is not displayed, choose it by selecting the SETTINGS-Analog command.

3 Choose the SETTINGS-No Title command to display the window without the title bar and menu. Bring back the Title bar and menu by double-clicking in the Clock window.

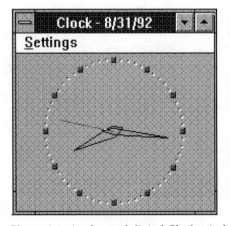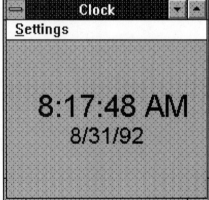

Figure 6.1 Analog and digital Clock windows.

4 Choose the SETTINGS-Seconds command to display the second hand on the traditional clock face. (If the seconds hand is already displayed, this step removes the seconds hand.)

5 Choose the SETTINGS-Date command to display the current date in the title bar of the analog Clock window. (If the date is already displayed, this step removes the date.)

6 Choose the SETTINGS-About Clock... command to view a dialog box showing program information associated with running the Clock accessory. Then click on the OK button to close the dialog box.

7 Choose the SETTINGS-Digital command to display the Clock in a digital format. Then choose the SETTINGS-Set Font... command to display the Font dialog box. Note the current font used to display the information in the Clock window. Select another font, and choose OK to see the changes in the Clock window. Repeat this procedure, then select the original font and move to the next step.

8 Choose the SETTINGS-Seconds and SETTINGS-Date commands, to return those settings to their original format, and note the changes in the Clock window.

9 Drag the title bar to different screen locations to verify that you can place the window where you choose.

10 Adjust the size of the Clock window into a two-inch square and place it inside the lower right corner of your Accessories window.

11 Click on the (larger) Accessories window to cover the Clock window.

NOTE: If the Always on Top command has already been selected from the (Clock) Control menu, the Clock window will still be displayed on top of the Accessories window. If this is the case, open the (Clock) Control menu and click on the Always on Top command to turn it off (and remove the checkmark placed in front of the command).

12 Press Ctrl+Esc (or double-click on an unoccupied space on the desktop) to show the Task List utility; then double-click on the name of the Clock accessory to redisplay the Clock window.

13 Click on the (Clock) Control-menu box to open the (Clock) Control menu, then choose the Always on Top command.

14 Click once on the Accessories window to make it active, and notice that the Clock window, although not active, still appears in the foreground of the desktop.

15 Click on the Control-menu box of the Clock window to make the window active and open its Control menu. Choose the Always on Top command to turn the option off.

16 Reduce the Clock window to an icon and then restore it.

17 Close the Clock window by double-clicking on its Control-menu box.

NOTE: To change the time/date displayed in the Clock window:

1. Open the Control Planel window (from the Program Manager Main window).

2. Double-click on the Date/Time icon to display the Date & Time dialog box.

3. Move to the appropriate text box and insert the proper date/time. Then choose OK to close the dialog box and initiate the changes.

4. Redisplay the Clock window to verify your changes.

5. Close the Control Panel window.

Calculator

The Calculator accessory operates in either the standard mode or the scientific mode. Most of your daily calculations can be completed with the standard calculator (see Figure 6.2), which displays the keys generally found on a small hand-held calculator. The Calculator window may not be sized; however, it may be moved, minimized, and restored.

To change to the scientific calculator, choose the VIEW-Scientific command from the menu bar. The scientific calculator includes all the functions of the standard calculator, along with 30+ programming, number-base, trigonometric, and statistical functions. The standard calculator is discussed in this text. For information regarding the scientific calculator, refer to your Windows documentation.

Entering Numbers and Symbols

To enter values, either click on the corresponding on-screen buttons or press the appropriate keys on the keyboard. When working with the Calculator accessory, many users prefer to use the keyboard (specifically the 10-key number pad) rather than the mouse.

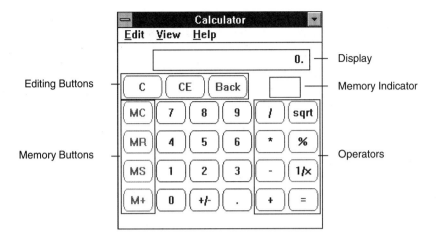

Figure 6.2 The standard calculator.

The basic procedure for entering a calculation consists of:

1. Enter the first number.

2. Enter the desired operator.

3. Enter the second number.

4. Enter the next operator and number (repeat as often as necessary), or complete the calculation by pressing Enter, the = key, or clicking on the = button.

In the following exercise you will use the standard calculator to determine the answers for some simple equations. Feel free to use the on-screen buttons, or the keyboard, to enter the numbers and operators. When you enter an equation consisting of three or more numbers, the display will show a temporary answer for the numbers and operations entered.

$\boxed{1}$ Load the Calculator accessory by double-clicking on its icon in the Accessories window. If necessary, choose the VIEW-Standard command to display the standard calculator.

TIP: Minimizing the other open windows on your desktop may make it easier for you to focus on the Calculator window.

$\boxed{2}$ Enter the equation, 4–1+2*6, in the following steps:

   a. Enter 4 – 1 + (the first part of the equation) then look at the display (it should show the number 3).

b. Enter the next number (the number 2) and the next operator (the *); the display will be updated to show the number 5 (4–1+2=5).

c. Enter the last number of the equation (6) and the = sign. The display should be updated to show 30 (the value of 5*6).

TIP: After completing one calculation, you may start a second calculation without clearing the old value from the display area. If you prefer to start with a 0 in the display space, either press Esc or choose the C button on the Calculator.

3 Without clearing the display, determine the answer to the following equation: 7*8–9+4/3. (The answer is 17).

4 Clear the display by clicking on the C button (or pressing Esc). Then determine the answer to the following equation: 5.25+6.37–8.95*4.77/999999999. (The answer is 0.00000001273590001274.)

5 Solve the following equation: 123456789*123456789. (The answer is 1.524157875019e+016.)

The answers to the last two problems indicate the range of numbers you can work with when using either the standard or scientific calculators. While the answer to step 4 is obviously a very small number, the answer to step 5 may be a little confusing. The answer to step 5 was displayed in scientific notation, because the actual number was too large to appear in the calculator's display area. The Calculator uses scientific notation to display any number larger than 9,999,999,999,999.

To repeat an operation, press the Enter key after the equation is completed. This action causes the last operation to be performed on the number currently being displayed.

When working with memory, the existing memory value remains the same between calculations, unless you clear it or make modifications to it. Values do not stay in memory after the Calculator has been closed. When the memory function is engaged, an M appears in the box located above the / and sqrt buttons.

Complete the following exercise to practice repeating an operation on a number in the display area and to practice working with the memory function.

1 Display the standard calculator, then enter the equation 97+3+2= (the answer is 102).

2 With 102 appearing in the display area, click on the on-screen = button (or press the Enter key once) to see the number change to 104. The number changes because this step causes +2 (the last operator and last number entered of the previous equation) to be reentered.

3 Repeat step 2 to change the number to 106.

4 Enter the number in the display area (106) into the Calculator's memory by clicking on the M+ button in the Calculator (or press Ctrl+P). Then clear the display area.

5 Multiply the number 2 by the value in memory by clicking on the following underlined items: 2 * the MR button =. (When you clicked on the MR button the number 106 should have appeared. The answer to this problem is 212.)

6 Clear the memory by clicking on the MC button. Enter the number 4 into the display area, then enter this value into the Calculator's memory.

7 Enter the following equation using the MR button: 100/MR button. This equation divides 100 by the value in the Calculator's memory (the answer is 25).

8 Press the Enter key to repeat the step of dividing the number in the display area by 4 (the new answer is 6.25).

9 Close the Calculator window.

Notepad

The Windows **Notepad** is a simple text editor that lets you create short (approximately 50,000 characters or less) notes, lists, or batch files. Notepad saves files in the ASCII (American Standard Code for Information Interchange) format, thus allowing most word processing software to load files created in Notepad. While it does not provide text-formatting options, Notepad does allow for changing words in text files. (Text files often have a .TXT extension.) The .TXT extension is associated with the Notepad accessory.

Start Notepad by double-clicking on its icon in the Accessories window. The initial Notepad window is shown in Figure 6.3.

Through your work with the previous chapters, you have already been exposed to the Notepad window. In the following brief exercise, you will open the Notepad window and learn to work with the **I-beam pointer** and the **insertion point,** two features found in most Windows programs that enable you to manipulate text.

1 Open the Accessories window inside the Program Manager window.

2 Double-click on the Notepad icon to open the Notepad window.

3 Size the Notepad window to expose some of the desktop or other windows, and leave the pointer outside the Notepad window.

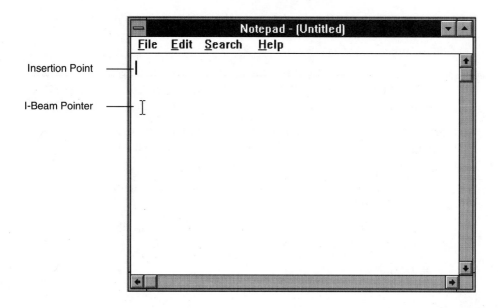

Figure 6.3 The initial Notepad window.

4 Watch the arrow pointer change to an I-beam pointer as you move the pointer inside the Notepad window work area. The I-beam-shaped pointer indicates that Windows is ready to accept text. Watch the I-beam pointer change back to the arrow pointer when you move it outside the Notepad window.

5 Note the location of the insertion point (the thin, blinking, vertical line in the work area of the window). This is the location where text will appear when it is keyed. In a new window, the insertion point is located in the upper-left corner of the work area.

NOTE: To edit a piece of text, you must first move the insertion point to the location of the text. Moving the insertion point to a new location is most commonly done by moving the I-beam pointer to the desired position and then clicking the mouse.

6 In your current (blank) Notepad window, try to move the insertion point by moving the I-beam to the middle of the window and clicking the mouse button. You can see that the insertion point does not move because no information (text, numbers, spaces, tabs) has been placed in the middle of the window yet. The I-beam must be located next to existing text (including a space) in order to move the insertion point.

As you look at the empty Notepad window, you see the vertical and horizontal scroll bars. Because there is no text to scroll to, the scroll bars are inactive at this time. After reading the next section on the FILE menu, you will enter text and see how the insertion point, I-beam, and scroll bars are used as you create various Notepad documents.

The FILE Menu

Most Windows applications have a FILE drop-down menu similar to the one in Notepad. This section examines the FILE commands as they apply to Notepad and most other Windows applications. The three basic groups of commands found in the FILE menu relate to moving files between disk and memory (New, Open, Save, Save As), printing commands (Print, Page Setup, Print Setup), and exiting the program (Exit). Listed below are the Notepad FILE commands and their functions.

Command	Function
New	Opens a blank window to allow for creating a fresh document. If the window is not empty, a warning message is displayed to allow for saving the current information before it is cleared from memory.
Open...	Displays a dialog box that enables the user to load an existing document.
Save	Saves the document under its existing name.
Save As...	Saves the document under a new name that the user creates in the accompanying dialog box.
Print	Prints the contents of the window.
Page Setup...	Enables the user to change the margins and create headers and footers for each page.
Print Setup...	Enables the user to select a printer and appropriate options.
Exit	Closes the window.

Creating and Saving a Document

You may create a document by simply keying in its contents. Once you key in the first three or four words, Notepad seems very much like a word processor.

However, as you reach the end of the first line and prepare to see the text automatically move to the second line, you may be surprised to see the first line continue past its normal length. In fact, as you continue keying, you'll see your first words scroll off the screen.

Word wrap is a function included in most word processors that instructs the computer to create the end-of-line breaks for you. The advantage of word wrap is that no words are split between lines (unless you use a hyphenation command). Notepad does not automatically use the word wrap function. If you want to activate the word wrap function, you must select it by choosing the EDIT-Word Wrap command.

A crucial component of the document creation process is frequently saving your file WHILE it is being created. Saving a document before it is completed is recommended to protect yourself from having to start completely from the beginning if something were to happen to the file you are working on (for instance, a brief power fluctuation that restarts your computer). Many computer users save their current file every 5 to 10 minutes.

In the following exercise you will learn to create a Notepad document, use the word wrap function, and save the file.

1 Enter the following paragraph into the Notepad window. (Use the backspace and cursor control keys to correct any mistakes.)

My favorite time of the year is summer. I enjoy being outdoors as much as possible. Playing tennis in the park is great exercise.

---

2 By the time you finished the last sentence, you probably noticed that your first sentence was scrolling off the left side of the Notepad window. Activate the word wrap function by choosing the EDIT-Word Wrap command. This wraps your text and removes the horizontal scroll bar from the bottom of the Notepad window. Your window may now look similar to Figure 6.4.

3 The insertion point should be located in front of the letter M in the first sentence. Move the I-beam pointer just past the period in the last sentence and click the mouse to relocate the insertion point. Press the spacebar twice, and then enter the following sentence to finish the paragraph:

A sunset walk along the beach is the best way to relax at the end of a summer's day.

Figure 6.4 Results of the Notepad EDIT-Word Wrap command.

4 In the following steps you will save this file on your Data Disk.

a. Choose the FILE-Save As... command to display the Save As dialog box (see Figure 6.5).

b. By default, the File Name text box is selected. Also by default, all Notepad files have a .TXT extension, unless a different extension is entered by the user.

Enter the file name SUMMER, but do not enter a . or extension. Do not press Enter.

c. Move the pointer to the Drives drop-down list box and select the drive that contains your Data Disk.

d. Move to the Directories list box, located above the Drives box, and double-click on the CH6 directory entry to open it. This is where you will save your file. The path listed above the Directories box should be similar to: a:\ch6.

e. Click on the OK button (or press Enter) to save the file.

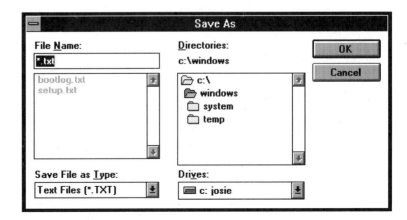

Figure 6.5 The Save As dialog box.

    f. Once the file is saved, you are returned to the Notepad window. The window title bar should now display "Notepad - SUMMER.TXT" to indicate the name of the current file.

5 Choose the FILE-New command to clear the window. (Because you just saved the file, you will not see a warning message to save the file, unless you accidentally pressed a key after completing step 4e. If the warning message appears, and you have already saved the file, choose No in the dialog box.)

6 Enter the following paragraph in a blank window. (Once you activate word wrap, it will stay on for the entire session, or until you turn it off.)

> I also like the winter, even though I am not too fond of the cold. Skiing is a good way to forget how cold it is. After a good day of skiing, I like to sit by a fire and have dinner with my friends.

7 Save this file as WINTER (let Notepad add the .TXT extension) in the CH6 directory on your disk.

8 Close the Notepad accessory by double-clicking on the Control-menu box.

Opening Previously Saved Documents

To place a previously saved file into a window you must "open" the file.

In the following exercise you will learn how to use the Open dialog box to display the documents you previously created with Notepad and how to save revisions made to existing files.

1 Open the Notepad accessory.

2 Choose the FILE-Open... command to display the Open dialog box.

3 Open the Drives drop-down list box and select the drive that contains your Data Disk (see Figure 6.6).

4 In the Directories list box, double-click on the CH6 directory to open the directory. Note that the SUMMER.TXT and WINTER.TXT files now appear in the Files list box.

NOTE: By default, only the files with a .TXT extension are initially located in the Notepad Open dialog box. Clicking on the List Files of Type drop-down list box, displays other options for listing available files in the Open dialog box.

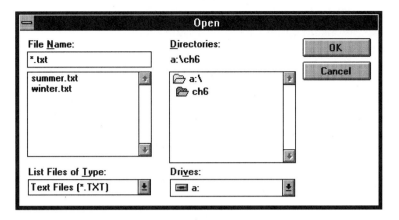

Figure 6.6 The Open dialog box.

5 Open the WINTER.TXT file either by double-clicking on its name in the File Name list box, or by selecting the file and choosing the OK button.

6 Because word wrap is not automatically activated, the document appears as one line extending past the window border. Choose the EDIT-Word Wrap command to show the entire document in the window.

7 Type your name at the beginning of the document, then press Enter twice.

8 Choose the FILE-Save As... command and name the file WINTREV (let Notepad add the .TXT extension). Notice the change in the Notepad title bar.

9 On the line below your name, enter today's date, then press Enter once.

10 Choose the FILE-Save command to save the revision of the file under the same name. Notice that when using the FILE-Save command you do not work with an accompanying dialog box (because the file has already been named).

11 Choose the FILE-New command to clear the Notepad window.

Selecting and Editing Text in Notepad

The process of selecting (also referred to as highlighting) data is a critical element in most Windows applications. Selected data is enclosed in a rectangle and generally appears in reverse print. When working in Notepad, the easiest way to select text is to use the mouse to complete the following steps:

1. Move the I-beam in front of the first character in the group to be selected and depress the mouse button.

2. Keep the mouse button depressed and drag the I-beam just past the last character of the group.

3. Release the button.

TIP: At times it may be more effective to use the steps listed above, but start at the end of the group and work toward the top of the document. Use whatever method is the most appropriate for you.

Practice using the Open, Save, and Save As... FILE commands and selecting and editing text by completing the following steps.

1 (If necessary, load Notepad, choose the FILE-Open... command, select the drive that contains your Data Disk, and open the CH6 directory.)
Open the WINTER.TXT file and activate the Word Wrap function.

2 Move the insertion point to the beginning of the third sentence (just in front of the word "After"). Then enter the following sentence:

Ice skating is fun too.

Notice how the existing text is moved to the right of the newly inserted text.

3 Select the word "also" in the first sentence (the second word of the document) and press the Delete key to remove the word. (When you edit a sentence by deleting a word, or group of words, remember to delete one space on one side of the selected text to keep proper spacing among the words in the sentence.)

4 Delete the entire sentence you added in step 2, then choose the FILE-Save As... command to name the revised file as WINTER1.TXT and save it under the CH6 directory on your Data Disk.

5 Open the SUMMER.TXT file. (Because the latest version of the WINTER1.TXT has been saved, this step will automatically clear WINTER1.TXT file from the Window.)

6 Select the first two words in the third sentence (Playing tennis). Then type the words "Roller skating" on top of the selected words. The words "Playing tennis" are deleted and replaced with "Roller skating". Save this file as SUMMER1.TXT.

7 | Reload the original SUMMER.TXT file. Move the insertion point to the beginning of the third sentence and press Enter twice.

8 | Choose the FILE-Save command. This results in the two-paragraph version of the file being saved as SUMMER.TXT. The original (one-paragraph) version has been erased.

9 | Choose the FILE-New command to clear the Notepad window.

Using the EDIT-Undo Command

The EDIT-Undo command enables you to reverse (or "take back") the *last* editing action you entered. Complete the steps below to practice using the EDIT-Undo command.

1 | (If necessary choose the FILE-Open... command, load Notepad. Select the drive that contains your Data Disk and open the CH6 directory.)
Open the WINTER1.TXT file and activate the word wrap function.

2 | Select the first sentence (I like the winter, ...) and then delete it by pressing the Delete key.

3 | Choose the EDIT-Undo command to return the sentence to its previous location.

4 | Start a new paragraph at the bottom of the document and enter the following sentence:
Steaming hot chocolate is my favorite winter beverage.

5 | Delete the word "Steaming" and capitalize the "h" in hot.

6 | Select the document's first sentence (I like the winter, ...) and delete it.

7 | Choose the EDIT-Undo command to bring back the first sentence and to try to reinstate the word "Steaming" at the beginning of the second paragraph. (You should not be able to bring back the word "Steaming." When you choose the EDIT-Undo command a second time, it removes the first sentence again.)

8 | Choose the FILE-Exit command to close the Notepad accessory. Do not save the changes to the WINTER1.TXT file.

Using the EDIT-Time/Date Command

To use Notepad to create a time-log to record how you spend your time:

1. At the left margin of a blank Notepad window, type .LOG.

2. Save the document under the desired name.

Each time you open this document, the current date and time (corresponding with your computer system's date and time settings) is added to the end of the document. You can then type a brief message explaining how you used your time since the last entry to this file.

To add the time and date to a Notepad document:

1. Move the insertion point to the location where you want the time and date entered.

2. Choose the EDIT-Time/Date command.

Printing the Documents

To print a Notepad file from the default printer:

1. Open the desired file.

2. Make sure your printer is on-line and ready.

3. Choose the FILE-Print command.

Calendar

The Calendar accessory is an electronic daily/monthly planner. Along with containing your recorded appointments in a day, date, and time format, the Calendar provides a visual and audio alarm which may be set to remind you of an upcoming event. Figure 6.7 illustrates the daily and monthly Calendar windows.

Opening Calendar and Changing Its Contents

To open the Calendar accessory, double-click on its icon in the Accessories window.

The current date and time displayed in the Calendar window corresponds with your system's date and time settings. Calendar's default setting is the daily view, with the day being divided into one-hour segments. To change to a window displaying an entire month, choose the VIEW-Month command.

To change the time interval, the hour format (12-hour clock with AM/PM listing or a 24-hour military clock), or the starting time for the daily view,

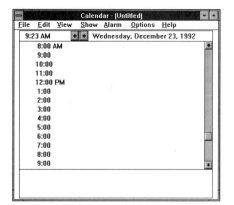

Figure 6.7 The daily and monthly Calendar windows.

choose the OPTIONS-Day Settings... command and select or enter the appropriate options in the Day Settings dialog box (see Figure 6.8).

Located just below the Calendar window VIEW and SHOW menu bar options are left and right scroll arrows. When in the daily view, each click on the left arrow moves the calendar back one day, while each click on the right arrow moves the calendar ahead one day. Clicking on an arrow, and keeping the mouse button depressed, scrolls the calendar many days at a time—just release the button when you see the desired date.

When in the monthly view, clicking on an arrow moves the window forward/backward an entire month at a time. Clicking on an arrow and keeping the mouse button depressed allows you to quickly move through many months.

Additional ways to change the date include:

1. Pressing Ctrl+Page Down to move forward, or Ctrl+Page Up to move back.

2. Choosing the SHOW-Next to move forward, or SHOW-Previous to move back.

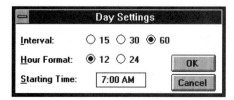

Figure 6.8 The Day Settings dialog box.

3. Choosing the SHOW-Date... command and entering the desired date in the Show Date dialog box. Use the mm/dd/yy format for entering the desired date. To return to the current date choose the SHOW-Today command.

Adding Unique Appointment Time Slots

Occasionally you may need to list a particular time that is normally not displayed in the daily view of the Calendar (for instance, 10:20 AM). To add unique time slots to the daily schedule, use the following commands:

1. Select the date of the appointment.

2. Choose the OPTIONS-Special Time... command to display the Special Time dialog box.

3. Insert the desired time (i.e., 10:20), select the AM or PM option, and click on the Insert button.

   To remove a time that was added with the OPTIONS-Special Time... command, repeat the steps listed above. However, choose the Delete button, instead of the Insert button, in step 3.

Entering and Removing Appointments

To enter an appointment:

1. Select the desired date (in the daily mode) and set the time intervals to the desired format.

2. Move the insertion point to the desired time and click once.

3. Key in the necessary information. If your information takes up more room than appears for the time line, the text will scroll from left to right as you continue to add characters. The maximum entry length is 80 characters. When you click on another time, the first part of the text is displayed. (Only one line per entry is shown.)

4. Most entries will fit in the allotted space. If an entry scrolls off the window, use the cursor keys to reveal the rest of the entry.

   To remove one appointment, select the text and then press the Delete key. To remove all appointments from a group of days:

1. Choose the EDIT-Remove... command to display the Remove dialog box.

2. Enter the first date in the From box. Enter the last date in the To box.

3. Click on the OK button (or press the ENTER key).

    To remove all the appointments from one day, repeat the above steps but leave the To box empty.

    Use the information given above to complete the following exercise of adding and removing appointments on your daily calendar.

1 Open the Accessories window inside the Program Manager. Open the Calendar accessory by double-clicking on its icon in the Accessories window.

2 If the day view of the Calendar is not displayed, choose the VIEW-Day command to display the day view.

    Move five days forward in the daily calendar by clicking five times on the right scroll arrow located just below the menu bar.

    Click 5 times on the left scroll arrow to return to today's date.

3 Use the SHOW-Date... command (or press F4) to show the daily schedule for Christmas Day, 1945. (Hint: Enter 12/25/45 in the Show Date text box.)

    After viewing the error message in the dialog box (you can view any day from January 1, 1980 to December 31, 2099), change the year to 1981 and try again. (You should see that Christmas was on a Friday in 1981.)

4 Move to today's date by using the SHOW-Today command.

5 Change to the month view and move forward a few months by using the right scroll arrow. Then use the SHOW-Today command to return to today's date.

6 Change the monthly view of the Calendar to next month, then select the first Monday of the month.

7 Change to the day view and enter a 1:00 PM shoulder doctor appointment.

8 Move forward one day and enter a 2:00 back doctor appointment on the Tuesday, then add the following appointments for the rest of the week. (When you finish, you will have entered five doctor appointments within five days.

Wednesday	3:00 PM	knee doctor
Thursday	4:00 PM	ankle doctor
Friday	5:00 PM	eye doctor

9 Return to the Monday on which you had a 1:00 PM shoulder doctor appointment and cancel the appointment.

10 Use the EDIT-Remove... command to cancel the remaining doctor appointments for the rest of the week.

Entering Notes

Near the bottom of the daily and monthly Calendar windows is an area for adding notes. Just select the date corresponding with the note, click in the note portion of the window, and enter the information. When that date is selected (in either the daily or monthly view), the note will be displayed in the lower section of the window.

Marking Dates

Sometimes you may want to mark certain dates to indicate special events, such as holidays. Choosing the OPTIONS-Mark... command displays the Day Markings dialog box (see Figure 6.9), which enables you to use five different symbols to mark different types of days. You can develop your own code for marking paydays, holidays, regularly scheduled meetings, or other events.

To mark a date (in either the monthly or daily view):

1. Select the date.

2. Choose the OPTIONS-Mark... command to display the Day Markings dialog box.

3. Click on the check box next to the desired symbol from the Day Markings dialog box and click on OK (or press the Enter key).

To remove a symbol from a date, select the date, open the Day Markings dialog box, click on the check box of the mark to be removed, and then choose OK.

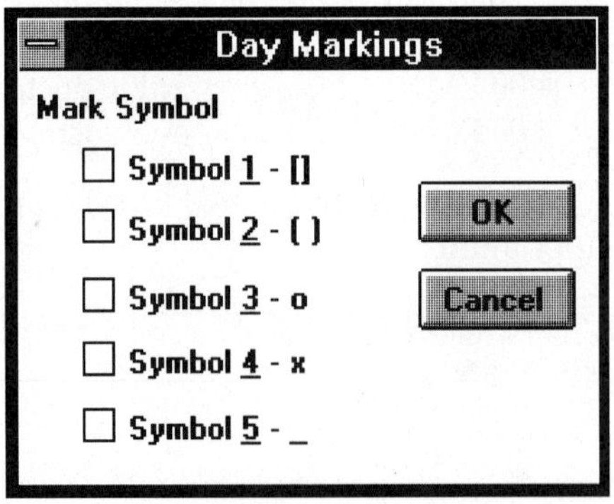

Figure 6.9   The Day Markings dialog box.

Setting Alarms

When using the *daily* planner, you can set an alarm to remind you of an appointment. To set an alarm, follow these steps:

1. Select the desired date.

2. Click on the desired time.

3. Choose the ALARM-Set command. (A bell symbol appears to the left of the selected time to indicate that the alarm is set.)

4. To be notified up to ten minutes before the appointment, and/or to use sound with the alarm, choose the ALARM-Controls... command to display the Alarm Controls dialog box (see Figure 6.10). Then complete the appropriate steps below.

   a. Enter the desired number of minutes, before the appointment, that you would like the alarm to be activated.

   b. Mark the Sound option box if you want a series of beeps (or other sounds, if your system is equipped to produce them) to indicate the alarm is activated.

   To remove an alarm setting repeat steps 1–3 above.

   At the assigned time, you hear a sound (if the sound is on) and then see the alarm message in one of the following ways:

   • If the Calendar is the active window, a box displaying the alarm message appears.

   • If the Calendar is a nonactive window, the Calendar title bar blinks. Once the Calendar is activated, the message is displayed.

   • If the Calendar has been reduced to an icon, the icon blinks. The message is displayed when the window is restored.

   • If a non-Windows application is being displayed, you may hear a sound (if the sound is enabled). However, you may not see the message until you leave the application.

   To turn the alarm off click on the OK button in the message box.

Figure 6.10 The Alarm Controls dialog box.

The Calendar FILE Menu

Except for the Print... command, the commands on the Calendar FILE menu function quite similarly to the commands on the Notepad FILE menu. A brief explanation of the Calendar FILE commands is given below:

Command	Function
New	Opens a new Calendar file. If changes have been made to the current calendar, a warning message is displayed to allow for saving the current information before the contents are erased.
Open	Displays a dialog box that enables the user to load an existing document.
Save	Saves the document under its existing name.
Save As...	Saves the document under a new name that the user creates in the accompanying dialog box.
Print	Opens a dialog box to enable the user to input the range of dates to be printed.
Page Setup...	Enables the user to change the margins and create headers and footers for each page.
Print Setup...	Enables the user to select a printer and appropriate options.
Exit	Closes the window.

Choosing the Calendar FILE-Print... command displays the Print dialog box (see Figure 6.11) that allows the user to input the range of dates to be printed in the From and To text boxes. After the desired dates have been entered, choose the OK button to initiate the printing procedure.

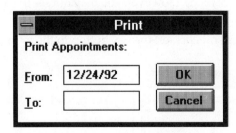

Figure 6.11 The (Calendar) Print dialog box.

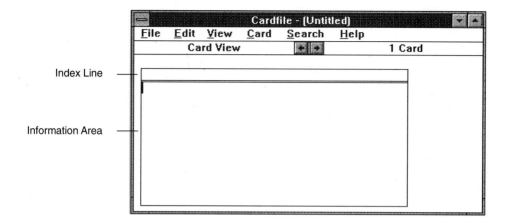

Index Line

Information Area

Figure 6.12 The initial Cardfile window.

Cardfile

The Cardfile accessory functions as an electronic stack of index cards. One of the most common uses for paper or electronic cardfiles is to provide a flexible list of names and corresponding addresses and phone numbers (and FAX numbers). When using Cardfile, you create your cards on the screen and then use the speed and accuracy of the computer to sort, review, and edit the stacks. If desired, you can display color pictures on your cards and print the cards. If your system is equipped with a modem, Cardfile can even enter phone numbers for you.

Opening Cardfile and Starting a New File

Open the Cardfile window (see Figure 6.12) by double-clicking on its icon (a row of index cards) in the Accessory window.

The Cardfile card includes a single index line (up to 40 characters) and an eleven-line information area. Cardfile automatically sorts the cards by the entry on the *index* line. Therefore, when creating a list of people, enter their last names first on the index line.

When the window opens, a new card appears with the insertion point placed in the information area of the card. Key points to remember when adding text to the information area include:

Figure 6.13 The Index dialog box.

- The order of the information does not affect the order of the cards. Place the information in a format that works best for you.

- The word wrap function is always turned on.

- You may add and delete text in the same manner as you did with the Notepad accessory. (After you learn to use the Clipboard, in the next chapter, you will also be able to copy and move information among the cards. However, Windows will not let you paste a document longer than 11 lines from the Clipboard into a card.)

After completing the information area on the first card, double-click on the card's index line (or choose the EDIT-Index... command) to display the Index dialog box (see Figure 6.13). Make your entry in the Index Line text box, and either press Enter or click on OK to return to the information area.

To change a card's index line: double-click on the index line, press F6, or choose the EDIT-Index command. When the dialog box appears, edit the entry and press Enter or choose OK.

After completing both sections of the card, you may start another card by pressing F7 (or by choosing the CARD-Add... command). When the Add dialog box appears, key the entry for the index line for the new card and press Enter, or choose OK.

The new card is then placed on top of the previous card. (The insertion point is located in the information area of the new card.) Depending on the size of the window work area, numerous cards, with their index lines revealed, are shown in a cascaded display.

Moving from Card to Card

There are numerous ways to look through your cards.

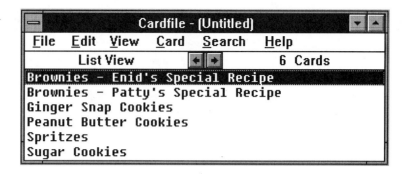

Figure 6.14 The Cardfile window after choosing the VIEW-List command.

Moving Forward or Backward

The ways to move forward or backward through the cards include:

1. Clicking on the left (backwards) and right (forward) scroll arrows appearing just below the SEARCH command on the menu bar. (Each clicks moves one card in the chosen direction.)

2. Pressing the Page Up key to move backwards one card, or pressing the Page Down key to move forward one card.

3. Pressing Ctrl+Home to move to the first card. Pressing Ctrl+End to move to the last card. Pressing CTRL+Shift+X (where X is a keyboard character) to move to the first card with an index line beginning with X. If two or more cards begin with the same character, continue to press CTRL+Shift+X to move to the desired card.

Using the VIEW Menu

The default setting for the Cardfile window displays a card. Choosing the VIEW-List command changes the window to display an alphabetical list of the index lines in the current file (see Figure 6.14). If the window does not display all of the index lines, use the scroll bars to reveal the remaining lines.

To move to a particular card from the List window, click on the desired index line and choose the VIEW-Card command.

Using the SEARCH Menu

Cardfile enables you to search for a particular card by searching the index lines or searching for keywords.

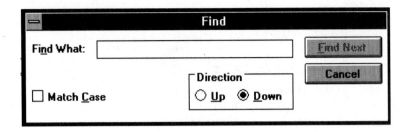

Figure 6.15   The Find dialog box.

To find a card by searching the *index lines:*

1. Choose the SEARCH-Go To... command (or press F4) to display the Go To dialog box.

2. Enter the desired index line and press Enter, or choose OK.

When the appropriate card is located, it is placed at the top of the stack. A dialog box indicates if no match is found.

To find a card through a keyword search of the information area:

1. Choose the VIEW-Card command (if the window is displaying a list of the index lines).

2. Choose SEARCH-Find... to display the Find dialog box (see Figure 6.15).

3. Enter the desired text in the Find What text box. Mark the Match Case option box, if needed. Choose the direction of the search. Click on the Find Next button.

4. After locating the desired card, click on the Cancel button or press ESC.

Saving and Opening Cardfile Files

Create as many cards as needed for a file. Use the FILE-Save As... command to initially save a related group of cards under one file name. You may decide to create a number of files to isolate various groups of information, such as business contacts, personal contacts, Christmas card lists, and recipe lists. Use the FILE-Open... command to recall a file previously saved. Upon reopening a file, you may view and edit information on various cards. If changes were made, save the file under its existing name by using the FILE-Save command. To create a new file, use the FILE-New command.

Complete the following exercise to practice creating and manipulating Cardfile files.

1 Open the Accessory window in Program Manager, then open the Cardfile accessory by double-clicking on its icon in the Accessory window.

2 In the information area, of the first card, enter the name and phone number of a person you would like to have lunch with on Monday. Then enter Monday on the index line for this card. Repeat this process for Tuesday through Friday.

3 Name this file LUNCH (let Cardfile add its own .CRD extension) and save it in the CH6 directory of your Data Disk.

4 Click on the Tuesday card to bring it to the top of the stack.

5 Move through the stack using the scroll arrows, the Page Up key, and the Page Down key.

6 Use the Ctrl+Shift+W key combination to bring the Wednesday card to the top of the stack. Repeat this process with the other cards; note what happens when you press Ctrl+Shift+T.

7 Use the SEARCH-Go To... command to display Friday's card on top of the stack.

8 Conduct a keyword search, looking for the last name of a person you will have lunch with. Repeat this step with a person's first name.

9 Clear the Cardfile window by choosing the FILE-New command.

Duplicating Cards

Sometimes, aside from minor changes, one card is a duplicate of another. The easiest way to duplicate a card is to use the CARD-Duplicate command. Just select the card, choose the CARD-Duplicate command and make the minor changes.

Restoring Cards

The EDIT-Undo command reverses only the last edit you made on a card. However, as long as you keep a card that is being modified on top of the stack, you may use the EDIT-Restore command to return a card to its original appearance regardless of the number of changes made to it. The EDIT-Restore command is unique to Cardfile.

Deleting Cards

To delete a card:

1. Move the desired card to the top of the stack.

2. Choose the CARD-Delete command to display a dialog box asking for confirmation of the delete command.

3. Press Enter, or click on the OK button.

Merging Files

At times, it is beneficial to merge two (or more) files into one larger file. Use the following steps to accomplish this task:

1. Open one of the files to be merged in the Cardfile window, then choose the FILE-Merge... command.

2. In the File Merge dialog box, select the name of the file to be merged into the open file, then choose OK, or press Enter. This merges the two files together and produces a new alphabetized listing of the cards. If two cards use the same index line, both cards are included.

3. Choose the FILE-Save As... command to give the merged file a new name. Or choose the FILE-Save command to remove the existing open file and replace it with the merged file.

Printing Files

The FILE menu has two print commands:

- The FILE-Print command prints the top card on the stack.
- The FILE-Print All command prints all the cards in the file.

Additional Accessories

Because most beginning Windows users tend to use the Terminal, Sound Recorder, and Media Player accessories less than the ones already discussed, only brief explanations of these accessories are presented. For more information on these accessories, review the corresponding sections in the Windows manuals.

NOTE: In the next three chapters, the Write, Recorder, Character Map, Paintbrush, and Object Packager accessories will be discussed.

Terminal

The Terminal accessory is a communications tool that enables computers to share information through the use of modems and the telephone system. The modem in the "sending" computer converts computer data into signals that can be sent through the phone lines to other computers with modems. The modem on the "receiving" computer translates the phone signals into data that a computer can work with. To run Terminal, you must have a modem installed in your system that meets the Windows 3.1 modem requirements (see your Windows 3.1 manual).

The Windows 3.1 Terminal accessory is significantly improved over previous Windows communications programs.

Sound Recorder

After installing a sound board in your system you may use the Sound Recorder accessory to record, play, and edit sound files. To effectively utilize the Sound Recorder, you will want to use headphones or external speakers.

Basically, sounds are vibrations that we hear and associate with meanings. Sound Recorder captures the vibrations and digitally stores them as files (with a WAV extension). Once captured, these files can be played back in their original state. They may be altered by changing the volume or speed, adding an echo, reversing the sound, changing the recorded pattern, or mixing with other sound files. Sound files may also be inserted into other types of Windows-based files.

Media Player

The Media Player accessory is designed along the lines of a compact disc player. It has a playback feature, but it does not have editing or special effects features (like the Sound Recorder). Provided you have the appropriate hardware and drivers, Media Player enables you to control: sounds stored in WAV files (i.e., Sound Recorder) or MIDI files, audio compact disks, animation, video disks, and other types of multimedia programs.

Summary

Windows includes a number of helpful accessory programs that may be utilized independently or in combination with other software programs. To access the various Windows accessories, open the Accessories window inside the Program Manager window; then double-click on the desired accessory icon(s). The general operating procedures for the Clock, Calculator, Notepad, Calendar, and Cardfile accessories were discussed in this chapter.

The **Clock** is the simplest accessory. The Clock window displays the time in either an analog or digital format. If desired you may display the current date, along with the time. You may also choose the SETTINGS-Always on Top command to ensure the Clock window is never covered by another window on your desktop.

The **Calculator** accessory may be displayed in the standard mode, which includes: the number keys; arithmetic function keys; square root, percentage, and inverse keys; and memory keys. Or, the Calculator may be displayed in the scientific mode, which includes all the keys in the standard calculator and additional advanced mathematical function keys. You may switch between the two modes by choosing the desired mode from the VIEW menu. To use either calculator, utilize the keyboard keys, or use the mouse to point-and-click on the appropriate buttons displayed in the Calculator window.

Notepad is a simple text editor that lets you create short notes and edit ASCII files. Although similar to a word processor, Notepad does not contain the formatting options commonly found in word processing programs. Notepad does include a special time-log feature that allows you to record the date and time on the files of your choice. You may want to use this feature for customer billing purposes or to keep track of phone calls. Unlike the Clock and Calculator accessories, the Notepad (and the Calendar and Cardfile accessories) allows you to save the information you created into files.

The **Calendar** accessory enables you to set up daily and monthly calendars for your appointments and meetings. When working in the daily calendar, you may determine the length of the time segments listed for each day (i.e., for most days you may use an hourly listing; however, on days when you have many appointments that are 20 minutes apart, you may display your entire workday in 20-minute segments). Sometimes you may want to mark your calendar with events that usually occur at the same time each month (like scheduled monthly meetings or paydays). To mark your calendar so you can quickly note a regular monthly occurrence, use the OPTIONS-Mark... command. The Calendar accessory also enables you to set an alarm to sound and display a dialog box that warns you of an upcoming event. Use the ALARM menu to set and remove an alarm.

The **Cardfile** accessory acts like an electronic Rolodex file. Each Cardfile card consists of an index line and an information area. The index line is used to contain the topic of the card (i.e., a person's name) and is the area of the card used to alphabetize the cards in the file. The information area includes up to eleven lines of text. One of the most common uses of the Cardfile accessory is for making a list of business contacts. Some of the Cardfile procedures discussed in this chapter included: the commands for duplicating cards, saving Cardfile files, merging numerous Cardfile files into one master file, and printing cards and files.

Applications

NOTE: When you are instructed to save files, save them in the CH6 directory of your Data Disk.

Application 1

1. Open the Notepad and use the Time/Date stamp to record the length of time needed to complete Application 2, Application 3, and Application 4. Identify the application by number, then record your start time, completion time, and any additional information specified in the application.

   After completing the time log for Application 4, save this Notepad document as CH6APP (let Notepad add its own extension) and print the file.

Application 2

1. Complete the following calculations with the standard calculator, and record your answers between the start and completion time on your Notepad document.

   a. 345*56*78/6524–24+7=?

   b. 5.34+6.75*9.894/3.6=?

   c. What is 53% of 4278?

Application 3

1. Open the Calendar accessory and set an alarm to sound in 4 minutes. When the alarm is activated, record on the Notepad document how far you have progressed on the remaining steps.

2. Design an hourly schedule for the coming weekend, starting with Friday night. (Some events may take more than one hour, so you need not have something different for each hour.)

3. Print your weekend schedule and save the file as WEEKEND (let Calendar add its own extension).

4. In your Notepad document, list the day of the week that the following holidays fall on in the year 1995: Valentine's Day, Christmas, and your birthday.

5. When the alarm sounds, turn it off. (If you finish steps 2 and 3 before the alarm sounds, wait for it to be sure it was properly set.)

Application 4

1. Open the Cardfile and create a birthday card list of at least four people. List the person's name in the index line and the present you would like to give that person in the information area. Let Cardfile add its own extension as you save the file as BCARD.

2. Print your file.

3. Make another file, of at least four people not included in step one, that you would like to study with. List the name in the index line and the subject you would study in the information area. Save this file as STUDY.CRD.

4. Merge the two files and save as PEOPLE.CRD, then print the merged file.

7

Write

Some people refer to Write, the Windows word processor, as an "executive" word processor because it can create most types of business communications and is so easy to use—even executives can learn to use it! Write does not include some of the advanced features found in the best-selling word processors, such as spell checking, a thesaurus, or mail merge functions, but it does enable you to create typical word-processed papers, such as memos, letters, and reports. Learning to use Write will serve as a valuable introduction to word processing in a graphical environment.

This chapter explains how to use Write to complete the four major word processing activities:

- creating—entering the text.
- editing—changing existing text and moving/copying text (through the Windows Clipboard).
- formatting—changing the arrangement or look of the text.
- printing—making a paper or "hard copy" of the text.

In addition to working with Write, you will also be exposed to the Windows Clipboard, the Character Map accessory, and the Recorder accessory.

The Write Window

Three symbols appear inside the initial Write window work area (see Figure 7.1). You are already familiar with the insertion point and the I-beam pointer. The third symbol, the small four-pointed box to the right of the insertion point, is the **end mark.** Each time a character is entered, the end mark advances so it is always the last item appearing inside the window work area. You hear a beep if you try to move the insertion point past the end mark.

Once a document has been paginated (broken into pages), the **page-status area,** located in the lower-left corner of the window, indicates the number of the page being displayed in the window. The page-status area continues to show "Page 1" until the document is paginated.

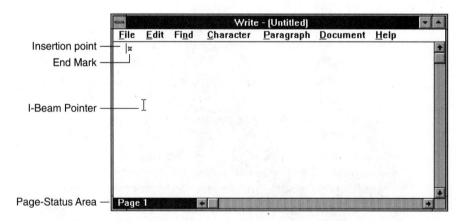

Figure 7.1 The initial Write window.

Editing the Text

This section examines the general steps of text editing, including: moving the insertion point to the appropriate location, selecting text, changing text, moving text, and copying text.

Moving the Insertion Point

You may move the insertion point through the use of the mouse or the keyboard. Use the familiar "point-and-click" mouse maneuver to place the insertion point at any location within the existing document. When necessary, manipulate the window scroll bars to display document text not currently on the screen.

Most of the cursor keys work in the expected manner. A list of shortcut keys for moving the insertion point follows.

Key Combination	Moves the Insertion Point to the...
Home	beginning of the current line
End	end of the current line
Page Up	next screen up
Page Down	next screen down
CTRL+Right Arrow	next word
CTRL+Left Arrow	previous word
CTRL+Page Up	top of the window
CTRL+Page Down	bottom of the window
CTRL+Home	start of the document
CTRL+End	end of the document

In the following exercise you will load a file and then edit it. To enter text, just key in the characters. Although the word wrap function is always activated, don't be surprised to see your text scroll off the side of the window. This may occur because of the size of your window. Write displays the number of characters per screen line that will appear when the document is printed (based on the current settings of the font, margins, and capabilities of the current printer). If necessary, adjust the borders of the window to display all the characters on a line.

1 Open the Program Manager.

2 Open the Accessories window.

3 Double-click on the Write accessory icon. (The icon includes the letter A, the tip of a fountain pen, and the label Write.)

4 When the Write window opens, choose the FILE-Open... command to display the Open dialog box.

If necessary, select the drive that contains your Data Disk, then select the CH7 directory.

Double-click on the CH7PRAC.WRI entry in the File Name list box to load the file into your Write window. Your Write window should now appear similar to the one in Figure 7.2.

5 The CH7PRAC.WRI file consists of two short paragraphs. In this step you will add two more paragraphs.

NOTE: When a document is opened, the insertion point is placed at the beginning of the first line. If you have accidently moved the insertion point, use the mouse or press Ctrl+Home to move the insertion point back to the beginning of the document.

Enter the following paragraph at the top of the document:

> This file is a revision of the CH7PRAC.WRI file that came with my Data Disk. I've added one paragraph to the top of the document and I'll add one more to the bottom.

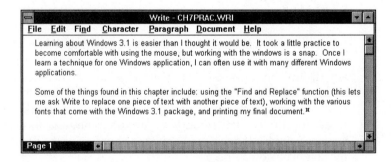

Figure 7.2 The Write window displaying the CH7PRAC.WRI file.

Press Enter twice at the end of the paragraph you just added. This will create a blank line between the first and second paragraphs.

6 Add the final paragraph to the document by following the steps below:

a. Move the insertion point into the last line of the document by moving the I-beam pointer into the last line and then clicking the mouse button.

b. Press the End key to move the insertion point to the end of the line. (Remember, the insertion point cannot be moved past the end mark.)

c. Press Enter twice to create a blank line between the existing paragraph and the next paragraph you are about to add.

d. Enter the following paragraph:

> Upon completing this chapter, I will have learned a number of ways to change the look of a document. With a little practice, I think I will enjoy using the Write word processor.

7 Use the FILE-Save-As... command to name your revision SAMPLE and save it in the CH7 directory on your Data Disk. (Write will add its own WRI extension to the end of the filename.)

Once the document is saved, its name appears in the Write window title bar. Your window should now appear similar to the one shown in Figure 7.3.

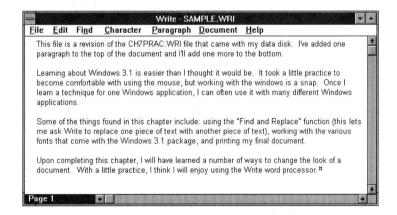

Figure 7.3 The Write window after completing the first exercise.

8 Leave the Write window displaying the SAMPLE.WRI file on your desktop and move to the next section.

The FIND Menu

The FIND menu provides a fast way to locate a certain word or phrase in your document. The commands on the FIND menu are explained below.

Command	Function
Find...	Displays a dialog box for inserting the word or phrase (up to 255 characters) to search for; includes options for matching the whole word and case.
Repeat Last Find (F3)	Repeats the previous find procedure.
Replace...	Displays a dialog box (see Figure 7.4) that includes both a Find What text box and a Replace With text box. The text inserted in the Replace With text box supplants the selected text located through the Find portion of the command. Start the process by choosing either the Find Next or Replace button. Check boxes let you designate matching the whole word and matching the case of the entry.
Go To Page...	Displays the Go To dialog box that contains the Page Number text box. Once the dialog box is displayed, enter the desired page number in the text box and press Enter (or choose OK) to move to the top of that page (the document must be paginated for this command to work properly).

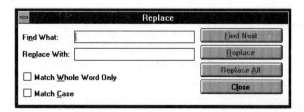

Figure 7.4 The Replace dialog box.

The buttons in the Replace dialog box are used as follows:

Command	Function
Find Next	Locates the next occurrence of the search text. To edit the text, press ALT+F6 to move to the document.
Replace	Replaces the specified text, then waits for the next command.
Replace All	Automatically replaces all the occurrences of the specified text throughout the document.
Replace Selection	Replaces the occurrences of the designated text only in the selected text on the document. (Supplants the Replace All button when a portion of text is selected.)
Close	Closes the dialog box.

Selecting Text

Although the Find and Replace function mentioned above is quite useful, there are often times when you may prefer to work directly in your document. Aside from adding or deleting individual characters, to change existing text you must first select the text and then make your edits. There are numerous ways to select text in Write.

To select one word, place the I-beam pointer on the word and double-click the mouse button.

One way to select a group of characters is to:

1. Place the I-beam pointer just in front of the desired text.

2. Depress the mouse button and drag the I-beam to the end of the text to be selected.

3. Release the mouse button.

To select a line of text or group of lines (often called a block), complete the following directions.

1. Place the pointer in the window *selection area*—the area that looks like a margin between the left window border and the text (see Figure 7.5). When the pointer is moved into this area it changes to an arrow pointing upwards and slanting to the right.

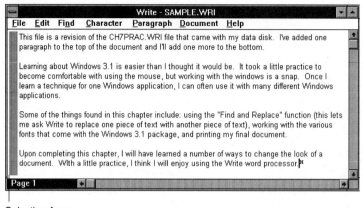

Selection Area

Figure 7.5   The selection area in a Write document.

2. Move the pointer (within the selection area) next to the first desired line, then to select...

a **line,** click once (the selected line will appear in reverse video).

a **group of lines,** click by the first line, then keeping the button depressed, drag the pointer down to the last line of the group, then release the button.

a **paragraph,** double click next to any line in the paragraph. To select multiple paragraphs: double-click by the first paragraph and, keeping the button depressed, drag down to the last paragraph, then release the button.

an **entire document,** hold down Ctrl and click.

To cancel a selection, click once in the work area.

Moving and Copying Text with the Clipboard Program

Using the Windows Clipboard allows you to move or copy data:

1. to different locations within the same document, or

2. from one document to another document.

Clipboard is actually a temporary storage area in memory. Data is copied from the source document to the Clipboard, and then copied from the Clipboard to the destination document.

The general procedures for using the Clipboard to move or copy information to either a different location in the same application window or to a document in another application window are listed below.

To *move* information:

1. Select the data to be moved.

2. Choose the EDIT-Cut command (to "cut" the data out of its current location and move it to the Clipboard).

3. Position the insertion point in the desired location of the document receiving the data from the Clipboard.

4. Choose the EDIT-Paste command to insert the data.

To *copy* information:

1. Select the data to be copied.

2. Choose the EDIT-Copy command (to "copy" the data to the Clipboard).

3. Position the insertion point in the desired location of the document receiving the data from the Clipboard.

4. Choose the EDIT-Paste command to insert the data.

Complete the steps below to practice using the Clipboard to move text within the same document.

1 If necessary, open the SAMPLE.WRI file in your Write window.

2 Select the second paragraph.

3 Choose the EDIT-Cut command. (Don't panic when the paragraph disappears from the window.)

4 Place the insertion point between the first and second sentences in the last paragraph.

5 Choose the EDIT-Paste command to insert the selected text at the insertion point.

NOTE: Do not make any adjustments to your text at this point. However, you should remember that when you move or copy sentences, you often will need to adjust the spacing at the beginning and end of the inserted text.

6 Return the last paragraph to its original format by choosing the EDIT-Undo command to undo the move. (While this action will undo the move, the text will not be reinserted to its original location unless you move the insertion point to the desired location and choose the EDIT-Paste command.)

| 7 | Modify steps 1–5 to create your own "copy-and-paste" combinations. Each time you cut or copy a new piece of data, the data previously stored on Clipboard is replaced. When you are finished, save the file as SAMPCUT.WRI in the CH7 directory of your Data Disk. |

TIP: Once data has been "cut" or "copied" to the Clipboard, it can be "pasted" an infinite number of times.

| 8 | Clear the Write window by choosing the FILE-New command. |

Except for the need to open more than one document, moving/copying data from one document to another follows the same basic steps as moving/copying data within the same document.

Generally, when using the Clipboard, you will not see a Clipboard window. However, double-clicking on the Clipboard Viewer icon, in the Main window, activates the Clipboard Viewer window. This window enables you to save the data on the Clipboard as a file and place this file into the appropriate drive and directory for future use.

Save Clipboard files by using the following steps:

1. Place the desired data on the Clipboard and start the Clipboard Viewer by double-clicking on its icon in the Program Manager Main window.

2. Choose the FILE-Save As... command and enter the desired name in the File Name text box. (Let Clipboard add its own .CLP extension when you complete step 3.) Then choose the desired drive and directory in which to save the file.

3. Choose OK.

To open Clipboard files, complete the following steps:

1. Display the clipboard viewer, then choose the FILE-Open... command.

2. Select the appropriate drive and directory in the Open dialog box.

3. Select the file in the File Name list box and choose OK.

To clear the Clipboard, complete the following steps:

1. When the file to be cleared is displayed in the Clipboard Viewer window, choose the EDIT-Delete command.

2. Choose Yes in the dialog box that appears asking if you want to clear the Clipboard. (Choosing No leaves the information on the Clipboard.) If the file was previously saved in Clipboard Viewer, you may re-load the file by using the procedure described above.

Formatting a Document

While editing changes the text in the document, formatting changes the appearance of the text. When formatting Write documents, you control the appearance of:

- the characters throughout the document,
- the spacing and alignment of the paragraphs, and
- the page layout of the document.

Formatting with the CHARACTER Menu

One of the primary reasons for formatting characters is to add emphasis to particular points in the text. The CHARACTER menu enables you to format the text of a Write document in a variety of ways. The commands on the CHARACTER menu are explained below.

Command	Function—Causes the selected text, or any text entered after this command, to appear:
Regular	in the default setting. (Shortcut key: F5)
Bold	in a thicker print. (Shortcut keys: CTRL+B)
Italic	slanted to the right. (Shortcut keys: CTRL+I)
Underline	underscored. (Shortcut keys: CTRL+U)
Superscript	raised one-half line above the regular text.
Subscript	lowered one-half line below the regular text.
Reduce Font	in the next available smaller size.
Enlarge Font	in the next available larger size.
Fonts	Displays a dialog box allowing the user to choose different fonts or font sizes (depending upon which fonts are installed and the printer capabilities).

You may use more than one format command for the same text. For example, one series of characters can appear in a bold, italicized, superscripted format. If the bold, italic, underline, superscript, or subscript commands have been chosen for the currently selected text, a check mark appears next to those commands when the CHARACTER drop-down menu is displayed.

To turn one of the commands off, select the command again. To return the selected text to the default setting, choose the CHARACTER-Regular command. (Choosing the CHARACTER-Regular command does not affect the selected text font or font size.)

Practice working with different character styles and changing the size of the font by completing the following exercise. Don't worry if you see some words move from one line to another as you complete the steps. Different fonts and character styles take varying amounts of space per letter.

1 Open the SAMPLE.WRI file in the Write window.

2 Drag the I-beam across the first four words of the first sentence of the document. Then choose the CHARACTER-Bold command to bold the selected text.

3 In the selection area (the area between the left window border and the text), place the pointer next to the word "Learning" at the beginning of the second paragraph. Click once to select the line and then press Ctrl+I (the shortcut keys) for italicizing selected text.

4 Use the selection area to select the second and third lines of the second paragraph, then press Ctrl+U to underline the selected text. Then move the insertion point to the end of the second paragraph. Your document should now appear similar to the one in Figure 7.6.

5 In the selection area, move the pointer next to the second line of the third paragraph and double-click to select the entire paragraph. Then enter the command to bold the selected text.

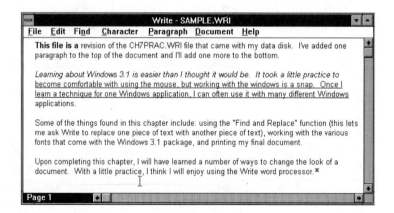

Figure 7.6 The SAMPLE.WRI document after completing steps 1–4.

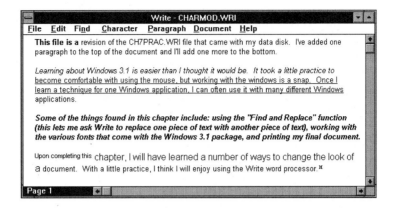

Figure 7.7 The CHARMOD.WRI document after completing steps 1–8.

6 | Select the first three words of the last paragraph, then choose the CHARAC-TER-Superscript command to show those words in a superscript format.

7 | Select the rest of the first line in the last paragraph, then choose the CHARAC-TER-Enlarge Font command to display the selected text in a larger font. (Notice that when you change font size, you often change the position of some of the text.) Move the insertion point to the end of the document.

8 | After studying your format modifications, save the file as CHARMOD.WRI on your disk.

Your document should now appear similar to the one shown in Figure 7.7.

9 | Place the pointer in the selection area and hold down the Ctrl key while clicking on the mouse to select the entire document. Then choose the CHARACTER-Regular command (or press F5) to change all the text back to the default setting EXCEPT for the text that is displayed in a larger font (remember, this command does not change the font size of selected text). Click anywhere in the work area to "deselect" the text.

Working with Fonts

A *typeface* is the basic design for a set of characters (letters, numbers, symbols, and punctuation marks). Helvetica and Courier are names of typefaces. A *typestyle* is a variation of the basic appearance of the typeface. The most common styles of a typeface are regular, bold, italic, and bold italic. The type size is commonly measured in points (one point equals $1/72$ of an inch). A *font* may be defined as a typeface in a particular size and style. Hence, Helvetica is a typeface; 12-point Helvetica bold is a font.

To select a particular font, choose the CHARACTER-Fonts... command to display the Font dialog box (see Figure 7.8). Make a selection from the drop-down Font list on the left side of the dialog box. Once a font is selected, its name appears in the Font text box and an example of the font is displayed in the Sample box. When a new font name, style, or size is chosen, the Sample box is updated.

Windows provides its own fonts, which are called TrueType fonts, when it is installed in your system. Normally, you also receive a number of fonts when you purchase and install your printer—these are referred to as printer fonts. (In the Font list box, Windows TrueType fonts are identified with a double-T icon; printer fonts are identified with an icon resembling a printer.) You may also purchase "third-party" fonts from many retail or mail-order computer equipment/supply firms. Some of the fonts included in the Font List box are system fonts—which are used to display Windows menus and dialog boxes, and which provide compatibility with earlier versions of Windows. System fonts do not always give an attractive printed output, and it is recommended that you not use these when creating your printed pages. When a system font is listed in the Font list box, no icon is placed next to its name.

Most users prefer using the Windows TrueType fonts (see Figure 7.9). These fonts appear on the screen in the exact way they will appear on the printed document. The True Type fonts that come with Windows 3.1 include the regular, bold, italic, and italic bold versions of the Arial, Courier New, and Times New Roman typefaces and regular versions of the Symbol and Wingdings typefaces.

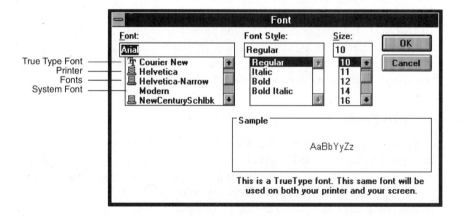

Figure 7.8 The Font dialog box.

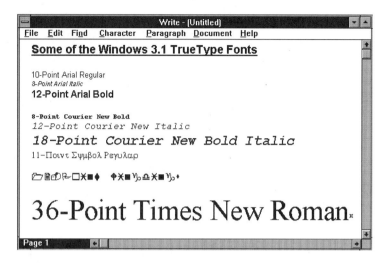

Figure 7.9   Some of the Windows TrueType fonts.

Character Map

Sometimes it may be beneficial to insert a few special characters to add emphasis to a particular point in your document. Character Map (see Figure 7.10) is an accessory that enables you (through the use of the Clipboard) to place characters and symbols from other character sets into your document.

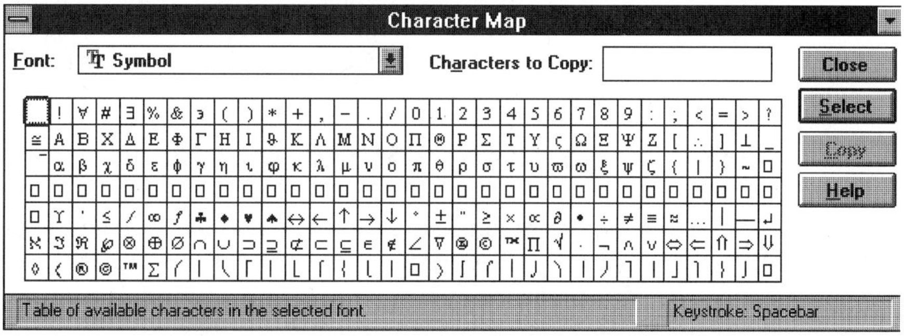

Figure 7.10   The Character Map window.

The Character Map window enables you to choose from the fonts available to your system by clicking on the Font drop-down list box. After selecting your font, the chart in the window displays how each of the characters appears.

The steps below explain the basic procedure for using the Character Map accessory and the Clipboard to insert characters into a document you are working with.

1. Determine the location in your document where you want to insert special characters, then open the Character Map accessory by double-clicking on its icon in the Accessories window.

2. Open the Font drop-down list box and click on the desired font. (If you are not sure which font to use, continue to click on a font and view the results until you are satisfied with the set being displayed.)

3. To see an enlargement of any character, move the pointer on top of the character and hold down the mouse button. When you select a character (by pointing and clicking on it) it is enclosed in a box to indicate it is the current choice.

4. To move characters to the Clipboard:

   a. Select a character.

   b. Click on the Select button. This action results in the character being placed in the Characters to Copy box. (Or you may place a character directly into the Characters to Copy box by double-clicking on it.)

   c. When all the characters you want to copy have been placed in the Characters to Copy box, click on the Copy button to place the characters on the Clipboard. (If you send one character at a time, each time one character is sent, it replaces the previous character.)

5. Return to the desired application window and place the insertion point in the appropriate location. Then choose the EDIT-Paste command to insert the characters from the Clipboard into the current document.

Formatting with the PARAGRAPH Menu

The alignment of text, line spacing, and the indentation of the lines comprise the paragraph formatting options in Write. To change the appearance of existing paragraphs:

- place the insertion point in the paragraph to be formatted and choose the desired PARAGRAPH menu command or,

- select the text to be formatted (often more than one paragraph), then choose the desired PARAGRAPH menu command.

If you choose to enter a paragraph format first, and then enter the text, the paragraphs will be displayed in the newly chosen format.

The commands on the PARAGRAPH drop-down menu are described below.

Command	Function
Normal	Single-spaces text and aligns it with the left margin.
Left	Aligns text with the left margin; the right margin appears ragged.
Centered	Centers the text between the left and right margins; both the left and right margins appear ragged.
Right	Aligns text with the right margin; the left margin appears ragged.
Justified	Aligns text with the left and right margins; both margins appear straight.
Single Space	Single-spaces the paragraph.
1½ Space	Inserts ½ (the height) of a blank line between the paragraph's text lines.
Double Space	Inserts one blank line between the paragraph's text lines.
Indents...	Displays a dialog box that allows the user to change the left, right, and first line indents.

NOTE: Mouse users may also change the appearance of the paragraphs by using the Ruler. For more information on the Ruler, see the section "Using the Document Ruler" later in this chapter.

All the PARAGRAPH commands (except Normal and Indents...) display a check mark next to their name on the PARAGRAPH drop-down menu when they are activated.

Practice formatting paragraphs by completing the following steps.

1 If necessary, open the Write accessory and the SAMPLE.WRI file.

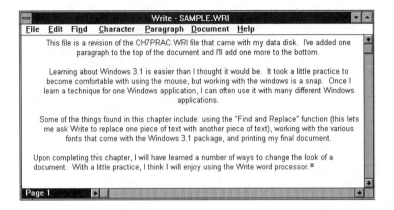

Figure 7.11   The SAMPLE.WRI file after completing steps 1–3.

2 Place the insertion point in the first paragraph and choose the PARAGRAPH-Right command. Note the changed appearance of the paragraph; the left margin is ragged and the right margin now appears straight.

3 Select the first three paragraphs. Then choose the PARAGRAPH-Centered command to view the paragraphs in a centered format. Your document should appear similar to the one in Figure 7.11.

4 Keep the first three paragraphs selected and complete the following steps:

   a. Choose the PARAGRAPH-Justified command to view the paragraphs with straight left and right margins.

   b. Choose the PARAGRAPH-Double Space command to view the paragraphs justified and double-spaced.

   c. Choose the PARAGRAPH-Single Space and the PARAGRAPH-Left commands to return the paragraphs to their original appearance. Then clear the Write window.

Choosing the PARAGRAPH-Indents... command displays the Indents dialog box (see Figure 7.12). Use this dialog box to indent entire paragraphs from the left and/or right margin, or to indent only the first line of a paragraph.

At first, working with indents can be a little confusing. The left indent starts as far to the left of the page as the margin will allow. For example, when printing a document with a left margin of one inch, even though the dialog box indicates the left indent is zero, the first character is printed one inch inside the left edge of the page (assuming the printer is properly prepared). If the left indent were changed to $1\frac{1}{2}$ inches, and the left margin remained at one inch,

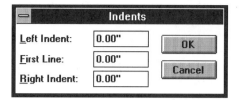

Figure 7.12 The Indents dialog box.

the first character on the page would appear 2½ inches inside the left edge of the paper.

If the left indent is changed to a number greater than zero, the first line indent can be:

a positive number—resulting in a first line being indented more than the rest of the paragraph;

remain at zero—resulting in the first line starting at the same location as the rest of the paragraph; or

a negative number—resulting in a first line being indented less than the rest of the paragraph—commonly referred to as a hanging indent.

NOTE: The ruler also lets you adjust the left, right, and first line indents. Indentation exercises are included in the "Using the Document Ruler" section later in this chapter.

Formatting with the DOCUMENT Menu

The DOCUMENT menu enables you to control the formatting options that affect the entire document. The DOCUMENT menu commands are explained below.

Command	Function
Header...	Displays the Header window which is used for entering the text of the header, and a Page Header dialog box which is used to set the header's distance from the top of the page, insert page numbers, clear all headers, set the header to appear on the first page, and return to the main document.

Footer...	Displays the Footer window which is used for entering the text of the footer, and a Page Footer dialog box which is used to set the footer's distance from the bottom of the page, insert page numbers, clear all footers, set the footer to appear on the first page, and return to the main document.
Ruler On	Displays a ruler, below the menu bar, to allow for setting tabs and indents, line spacing, and paragraph alignment with the mouse.
Tabs...	Displays a dialog box used for setting and removing left-aligned and decimal tabs.
Page Layout...	Displays a dialog box used for setting the starting page number, margins, and the measurement system.

Using the Document Ruler

The Ruler (see Figure 7.13) looks like a standard ruler that is placed just below the window's menu bar. Included on the Ruler are measurement values and icons used to view and control tab stops, line spacing, paragraph alignment, and indents.

NOTE: In Figure 7.13, the first-line indent marker has been placed to the right of the left-indent marker. If you place the insertion point in a paragraph that begins next to the left margin, and then activate the Ruler, the first-line indent marker may appear in reverse color inside of the left-indent marker.

To turn the Ruler on, choose the DOCUMENT-Ruler On command. To turn the Ruler off, choose the DOCUMENT-Ruler Off command.

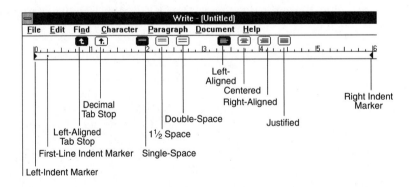

Figure 7.13 The Ruler.

Because the Ruler makes it easy to complete a number of formatting functions, many users prefer to leave the Ruler turned on whenever they are using Write. Although the DOCUMENT-Tabs command can be used to display a dialog box used for setting tab stops, we will examine how the Ruler can provide a more visual method for setting tabs.

By default, Write has tab stops every half-inch along a text line; these do not appear on the Ruler. Users may add 12 more tab stops; user-added tab stops do appear on the Ruler. As a tab stop is added, it cancels the *default* tab stops to the left of the newly added tab. The standard tab stop produces left-aligned text at the position of the tab stop. The left-aligned tab stop is automatically selected when the Ruler is first displayed. (The background for the selected tab—left-aligned or decimal—is darkened to indicate it is the selected tab.)

The decimal tab stop is used to neatly display a column of numbers. When using a decimal tab stop to format a column of numbers, the decimal points align at the tab stop; the whole numbers appear to the left and the fractional portions appear to the right of the decimal points.

To set left-aligned tab stops:

1. Place the pointer on the line under the Ruler measurements, at the location where the tab stop is to be entered, and click.

   To set decimal tab stops:

1. Click on the decimal tab stop icon. Refer to Figure 7.13 to differentiate between the left-aligned tab—which has a curved arrow stem—and the decimal tab—which includes a period to the right of a straight arrow stem.

2. Place the pointer on the line under the Ruler measurements, at the location where the tab stop is to be entered, and click.

   To change a tab stop:

1. Drag the tab stop to its new location along the Ruler, then release the mouse button.

   To remove a tab stop:

1. Drag the tab stop a few lines below the Ruler and release the mouse button.

   Paragraph line spacing and alignment may also be set from the Ruler. (Refer to Figure 7.13 to identify the icons corresponding to the line spacing and alignment options.)

   To set paragraph line spacing:

1. Move the insertion point inside the paragraph to be formatted.

2. Click on the icon representing the desired line spacing.

To set the paragraph alignment:

1. Move the insertion point inside the paragraph to be formatted.

2. Click on the icon representing the desired alignment.

The Ruler may also be used to change the paragraph indentation. To adjust the paragraph indentation:

1. Place the insertion point in the paragraph to be changed.

2. Drag the left- and right-indent markers (left and right arrowheads) and the first-line indent marker (the tiny solid square below the Ruler markings) to the desired position along the line located below the measurement marks on the Ruler. (See Figure 7.13.)

NOTE: To change the left indent, when the first-line indent marker is located inside the left-indent marker:

1. Drag the first-line indent marker a short distance to the right of the indent marker and release the mouse button. (This causes the first line of the paragraph containing the insertion point to be indented to the point where the first-line marker is located.)

2. The left indent marker should now appear solid. At this point, you may drag the marker to a new location.

Document Formatting Exercises

Complete the following exercise to practice using the Ruler to format a document.

1 If necessary, start the Write accessory and open the SAMPLE.WRI file from your Data Disk. Make sure the insertion point is at the beginning of the document.

2 Display the Ruler by choosing the DOCUMENT-Ruler On command. Move the first-line indent marker to the one-inch mark of the ruler and watch the first line of the first paragraph be indented one inch.

3 Set a left-aligned tab at the $1\frac{3}{4}$-inch mark. Then, with the insertion point in front of the first paragraph, press Tab once to see the first line indented $1\frac{3}{4}$ inches.

4 Set a left-aligned tab stop at the $1\frac{1}{4}$-inch mark. As soon as you release the mouse button, the text jumps back to the $1\frac{1}{4}$-inch mark (because you have pressed Tab only once). Press Tab again to move the first character to the $1\frac{3}{4}$-inch mark.

5 Move the left-indent marker to the ½-inch mark and notice how the text in the first paragraph shifts again. After you complete this step, your document will appear similar to the one in Figure 7.14.

TIP: Note that after you complete this step, the text lines up underneath the widest part of the left-indent marker.

6 Move the insertion point to the beginning of the second paragraph. Notice that the left-indent marker and the first-line indent marker have returned to their original locations.

7 Add three more left-aligned tabs across the Ruler. Then press the TAB enough times to test all your tab settings.

8 Select the third paragraph. Set the first-line indent marker and the left-indent marker at the 2-inch mark. (This will require two dragging actions. The first dragging action moves only the first-line indent marker.)

Drag the right-indent marker in to the 5-inch mark. (You may need to use the horizontal scroll bar to slightly reposition the text in your window to expose the right-indent marker.) Notice how your selected text is repositioned to correspond with the new indentations.

9 Move the insertion point into the second paragraph and complete the following:

a. Click on the icon to use the 1½-line spacing option.

b. Click on the icon to double-space the paragraph.

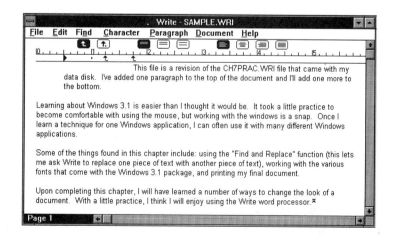

Figure 7.14   The SAMPLE.WRI document after completing steps 1–5.

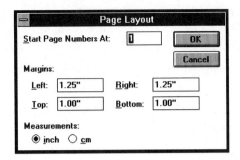

Figure 7.15 The Page Layout dialog box.

c. Click on the icon to single-space the paragraph.

d. Click on the icon to center the paragraph.

10 Save this document as SAMPLE2.WRI.

Determining the Page Layout

Choosing the DOCUMENT-Page Layout... command opens the Page Layout dialog box (see Figure 7.15). This dialog box helps you control the basic appearance of your printed output as it is used to set the page margins and starting page number for your document.

The default settings are shown in Figure 7.15. To start at a different page number, or use different margins, move to the corresponding text box and enter the new values. To work in centimeters instead of inches, click on the cm option button.

Paginating a Document

Paginating a document breaks it into pages based on the length of the text and the entries made in the Page Layout dialog box. You may paginate a document as often as needed. For short documents, you may prefer to let the pagination automatically take place through the printing procedure.

To view how your initial page breaks will appear, before printing the document, use the following steps.

1. Choose the FILE-Repaginate... command to display the Repaginate Document dialog box.

   To confirm each page break, mark the Confirm Page Breaks check box (see note below). If you do not want to confirm the page breaks, leave the box blank.

2. Click on OK, or press Enter.

3. If you chose not to confirm each page break, you may use the window scroll bars, or the shortcut keys discussed earlier, to move through the pages of your document.

NOTE: Choosing to confirm each page break causes another dialog box to appear each time Write is about to create a page break. This second dialog box lets you click on an Up button to raise the page break (you may not lower it). A Down button is included to let you move a page break down if it was raised. After positioning the page break at the desired location, click on the Confirm button.

As you move through a paginated document, its page numbers are displayed in the page-status area (in the lower-left portion of the window). A double arrowhead (>>) is displayed in the selection area of the window to indicate the start of a new page.

There may be times when you want page breaks to occur at particular places in the document (i.e., to avoid splitting tables or illustrations onto two pages). To manually insert a page break:

1. Position the insertion point in the desired location.

2. Hold down the Ctrl key and press Enter. This creates a dotted line across the document to represent a manual page break.

TIP: Remember that if you insert a page break into a previously paginated document, the new page break may affect the position of the remaining page breaks. Therefore, before printing, make sure to view the document on your screen to see if the remaining pages break in the desired locations.

Page breaks can be selected, deleted, or copied just as any other character in a document.

The Recorder Accessory

The purpose of the Recorder accessory is to enable you to record a series of commonly used keystrokes (and mouse movements) and then play them back (when needed) by pressing a key-combination. This series of keystrokes is referred to as a macro. One of the most useful times to use macros is when you design formats to use with particular types of documents (such as setting unique margins for various business memos or creating a commonly used header or footer for your documents). You may also use macros to enter lines of text that you often use in your correspondence, such as your return address.

In the exercise below you will use the Recorder to create a macro to display your return address for documents created in Write. In addition to Write, the Recorder can also be used with other Windows applications.

TIP: Because of the fluid nature of Windows and the ever-changing desktop, it is recommended that you use keyboard commands instead of mouse movements and restrict your macros to one application at a time when you first use the Recorder. Once the Recorder is started, it automatically returns to the most recently active window, therefore be careful not to click an unnecessary window before starting the Recorder.

Figure 7.16 shows the initial Recorder window that is opened when you double-click on the Recorder icon in the Program Manager Accessories window. The (Recorder) FILE menu enables you to open and save macros and merge macros from other files. The MACRO menu provides the means for recording, running, deleting, and changing the properties of a macro. The OPTIONS menu lets you control the Recorder default settings.

1 Minimize all windows except the Program Manager displaying the Accessories window and the Write window. Adjust the Program Manager window to cover the left side of the desktop, making sure the Recorder icon is visible. (The icon looks like a video camcorder with two cassette tapes.) Adjust the Write window to cover the right side of the desktop. Inside the Write window, choose the FILE-New command to display a fresh document window. Leave the bottom two inches of the desktop exposed so that program icons may be made visible.

2 Open the Recorder window by double-clicking on the Recorder icon in the Program Manager Accessories window and position it on the left side of your desktop. (Leave the bottom two inches of the desktop exposed.) Then choose the MACRO-Record... command to display the Record Macro dialog box (see Figure 7.17).

3 In the Record Macro Name text box key: Return Address.

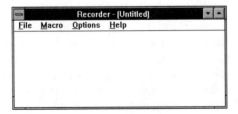

Figure 7.16 The Recorder window.

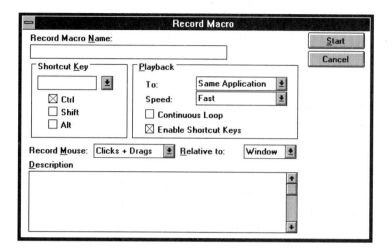

Figure 7.17   The Record Macro dialog box.

4   Click on the down arrow in the Shortcut Key drop-down list box to display the list of keys, then click on the Backspace key. (This assigns the Ctrl+Backspace key combination to your macro.)

5   Click on the Start button or press Enter to begin recording your macro. From this point, each keystroke will be recorded until you press Ctrl+Break.

6   As you start recording your macro, the Recorder window is reduced to a flashing icon to indicate it is recording your macro. At this point, if the Write window is not active, you need to make it active, then enter your name and address in the Write window.

7   After completing your entry (be sure to press Enter once following your zip code), press Ctrl+Break to stop recording and to display the dialog box shown in Figure 7.18.

8   To save the macro, select the Save Macro option and click on OK (or press Enter). This step causes the Recorder icon to stop blinking.

9   Restore the Recorder window to see the key combination and name of your new macro displayed in the window work area. (You may need to enlarge the Recorder window to see all the information, or you may use the window's scroll bars.)

10   Save the macro by choosing the (Recorder) FILE-Save As... command. Choose the proper drive and the CH7 directory to save your macro to your Data Disk.

Figure 7.18 The dialog box used for saving macros.

Then enter WRIRETAD (acronym for Write-return address macro) in the File Name text box and choose OK. (Recorder files have an REC extension.)

11 Minimize the Recorder window. (For macros to run, the Recorder window must either be open or minimized on the desktop.)

12 Clear your Write window without saving the changes and execute the macro in a new window by pressing Ctrl+Backspace.

13 Close the Recorder accessory and exit Write without saving your document.

NOTE: This exercise was intended to provide a brief introduction to the Recorder. For more information on this useful accessory, refer to the Windows Help facility.

Printing the Document

To print a document, choose the FILE-Print... command to display the Print dialog box (see Figure 7.19).

The default printer is listed near the top of the dialog box. If you need to change printers, choose the Setup... button to display the Print Setup dialog box. Click on the down arrow by the Specific Printer drop-down list box and select the desired printer. Then choose the Options... button to complete the printer change and return to the Print dialog box.

The Print Range box includes the following options:

All prints all the pages of the document.

Selection prints selected text in the document.

Pages allows user to enter starting and ending pages to be printed.

The Print Quality text box enables you to select the quality of the printed output (the larger the dpi number, the better the quality of output).

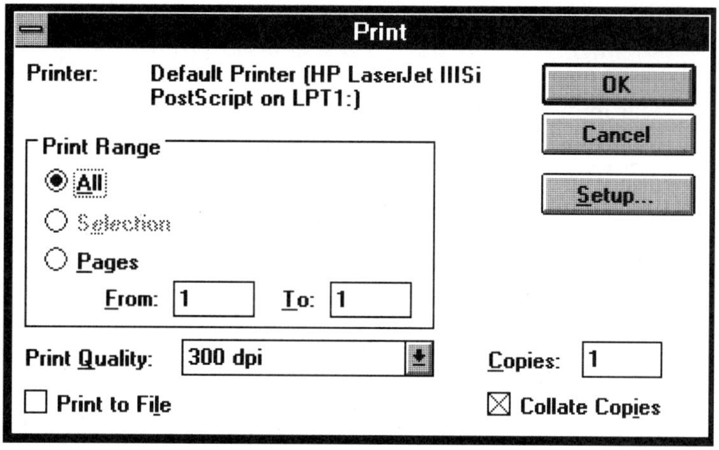

Figure 7.19 The Print dialog box.

The Print to File check box enables you to send the printout to another file instead of to the printer. (This command is most often used by people wanting to use a printer not currently available to them. They usually take the disk containing the printed file to another computer that is connected to the desired printer and then use MS-DOS commands to print the file.)

The default number of copies to be printed is one. The Copies text box allows you to change this number.

The Collate Copies command (if supported by your printer) separates each document page when printing more than one copy.

Clicking on the Setup button displays a dialog box used to prepare another (attached) printer to print your document.

Clicking on the Cancel button, voids any new settings you entered into the dialog box.

Clicking on the OK button (or pressing Enter) activates the printing process.

Summary

This chapter has discussed the use of Write, the Windows word processor. Write is often referred to as an "executive" word processor. It can be used to complete most business and daily word processing needs. However, it does not include all the advanced functions (i.e., spell-checking, merging, and using a thesaurus) of the full-featured word processors. While Write may not become the only word processor you will use, learning to work with Write has been a good introduction to word processing in a graphical environment. The full-featured, Windows-based word processors operate in a similar manner to Write, so you already have a head start in learning one of those packages.

Key components of the Write window include the standard window elements and the insertion point, end mark, page-status area, and selection area. The **insertion point** marks the location in the window work area where characters will next be entered through keyboard or mouse actions. The **end mark,** a small four-pointed box, appears after the last character of the document to indicate the end of the document. The **page-status area** displays the number of the page being displayed in the window. The page-status area continues to display "Page 1" until the document is paginated. The **selection area** is located between the left window border and the first characters in the lines of text. When the pointer is placed in the text area of the window it appears as an I-beam pointer; however, when the pointer is placed in the selection area it appears as a right-slanted, upward pointing arrow to indicate that it can be used to select lines or paragraphs of text.

The **functions of the Write FILE menu** include: opening blank document windows to allow for creating new documents, opening existing documents, saving files under new or existing names, setting up the printer, printing files, repaginating a document, and exiting the program.

The **Windows Clipboard,** a temporary storage area, holds data cut or copied from a source document. This data may then be placed into the same or different document(s). It is also possible to save information placed on the Clipboard, although the Clipboard is more commonly used as a temporary storage location during document creation and editing.

The **EDIT menu** enables the user to undo a previous edit, cut or copy information to the Windows Clipboard, paste information from the Clipboard, link information between documents, and move and size pictures placed in Write documents.

The **FIND menu** enables the user to conduct typical word processing search actions, search-and-replace activities, and to move to a particular page in a document.

The **CHARACTER menu** enables the user to enter or change the characters of the document to appear in: regular, bold, italic, underline, superscript, or subscript formats (or various combinations of formats, such as bold italic); various sizes; or various typefaces. (Windows refers to typefaces as Fonts, such as the Courier font.)

One way to insert special characters into a Windows document is to use the Character Map accessory and the Clipboard. The **Character Map** displays characters not found on most keyboards and the characters of various symbol fonts. The user opens the Character Map and copies the desired characters to the Clipboard; then the user returns to the original program and pastes the special characters from the Clipboard into the document.

The **PARAGRAPH menu** enables the user to format paragraphs as left aligned, centered, right aligned, or justified. This menu provides three spacing options: single space, 1½ space, or double space. Choosing the PARAGRAPH-Normal command returns the selected paragraph(s) to the left aligned and single spaced format. This menu also allows for changing the left, right, and first-line indents of one or more paragraphs.

The PARAGRAPH menu commands listed above, along with setting tabs, may also be accomplished through using the Ruler. Choosing the **DOCU-MENT-Ruler On** command displays the Ruler immediately below the menu bar. The Ruler contains icons corresponding to the commands in the PARA-GRAPH menu, along with icons representing left and decimal tab stops. The ruler also displays measurement values (either in inches or centimeters) immediately below the menu bar.

Along with providing access to the Ruler, the **DOCUMENT menu** also enables the user to work with headers, footers, tabs, page margins, and the program's measurement system.

The **Recorder** is the Windows accessory used for recording macros. Macros may be referred to as a series of predefined keystrokes. Mouse actions may also be included in the macros; however, in this chapter's introduction to the Recorder, only keystrokes have been discussed. The Recorder has been discussed in this chapter to show how certain items, such as a return address, lend themselves to being included in macros. The Recorder may be used with Write and many other Windows applications.

Applications

Application 1

1. Use Write to create a single-spaced, word-processed letter to your instructor, explaining some of the things you have learned in this chapter. Follow the structure given below to construct your letter:

   a. The first paragraph should contain the following *character formats*—bolded text, italicized text, underlined text, bold and underlined text, text in an enlarged font, and text in a reduced font.

   b. Create the second paragraph, and then use Clipboard to place three additional copies of the paragraph below the original. (Make sure to include a blank line between the paragraphs.) The original second paragraph should be left-aligned and single-spaced. Format the copies of the paragraph as follows:

1st copy—right-aligned, 1½-spaced
2nd copy—centered, single-spaced
3rd copy—justified, double-spaced.

c. Insert a tab stop at the 0.75 inch mark and start each paragraph with that tab stop.

d. Move the insertion point to the bottom of your document and start a new paragraph (left-aligned, single-spaced). Enter the following sentence:

A decimal tab was used to form the column of numbers shown below.

Enter a decimal tab at the two-inch mark of the ruler. Immediately below the new sentence, use the decimal tab and the following numbers to create a column of numbers: 2.7543, 131.60, 14.213, 5.67003, 32.65, and 481.325.

e. Change the top, bottom, left, and right margins to 1.75 inches.

f. Create a line under the numbers entered in step 1d. Then open the Calculator to find the answer to this addition problem and use the Clipboard to copy the answer from the Calcultor into your Write document.

g. Use the find-and-replace feature to replace the word "the" with "THE" throughout your entire document.

h. Save the file in the CH7 directory of your exercise disk as LETTER.WRI and print the document.

2. Circle and identify (in ink) each of the format options you used to create the document.

8

Paintbrush

The Paintbrush accessory provides the tools for creating drawings with your computer. People have used Paintbrush for creating greeting cards, floor plans, and a multitude of other images. We will focus on creating and editing simple illustrations in this chapter.

The tools you will learn to use are common to virtually all Windows paint and design programs. You'll probably find the icons are quite intuitive and that it is rather easy to create a drawing. Pointing devices, like the mouse, are the dominant method for creating illustrations in this type of program. Most of the chapter concentrates on mouse commands, although some keyboard commands are mentioned. Paintbrush is one of the few programs to use both the left and right mouse buttons. When the right button is needed, the text specifies the right button; otherwise, all references refer to the left button.

Starting Paintbrush

The initial Paintbrush window (see Figure 8.1) includes the familiar items, such as: the title bar, Control-menu box, sizing buttons, menu bar, borders, and scroll bars. The new elements in the Paintbrush window include the:

Drawing area The area where the images are drawn. The amount of computer memory and the type of monitor (and adaptor card) being used determine the initial size of the drawing area.

NOTE: Paintbrush is one of the most resource-intensive modules of the Windows package. The variables that most affect the performance of the Paintbrush accessory include:

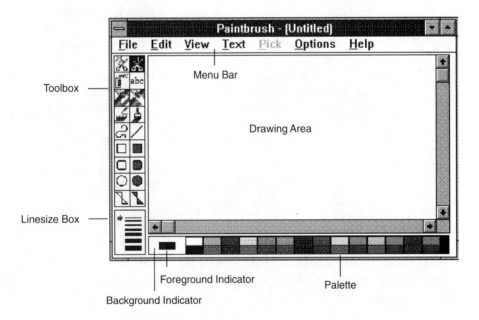

Figure 8.1 The initial Paintbrush window.

1. The amount of memory (RAM) in your system. Although Windows will run with less, most users prefer a minimum of 4 megabytes of RAM.

2. The monitor and video card used to display your images. Color VGA (video graphics array) or Super-VGA (super video graphics array) monitors, along with corresponding video cards in the system unit, are the monitors of choice because of their ability to show many colors at the same time, while also displaying a sharp resolution.

3. The type (and speed) of the central processing unit (CPU). Because working with graphics requires the CPU to make many more decisions than are usually completed when working with ordinary text, seeing the results of editing your drawings may take a little longer than seeing the changes when you edit text.

Toolbox   The area along the left side of the window containing the tools to create and edit your drawings.

Palette   The area along the bottom of the window containing the colors or patterns used to shade the foreground and background of the drawing.

Foreground/Background Indicator   The box to the left of the Palette which shows the selected foreground (inner box) and background (outer box) palette choices.

Linesize Box   The box in the lower-left corner of the window which enables the user to change to any of the line widths displayed in the box.

Open the Paintbrush accessory now by following the steps below.

1 Open the Accessory window inside the Program Manager window.

2 Double-click on the Paintbrush icon to open the Paintbrush accessory. (The icon looks like a painter's palette with the term "Paintbrush" displayed below it.)

The initial default selections for the Paintbrush window (when using a color monitor) include: the Brush tool, a thin drawing line, black foreground color, and white background color.

The Toolbox

The Brush is just one of the many tools included in the Paintbrush Toolbox. The cursor (or pointer), for the majority of the tools, appears as a crosshairs symbol (this looks like a large addition symbol). Figure 8.2 displays the icons, names, and corresponding cursors for the tools in the Toolbox.

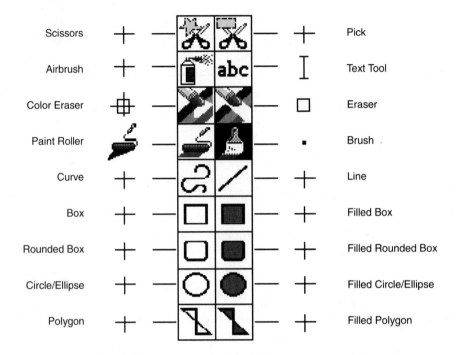

Figure 8.2 Toolbox icons, names, and cursors.

The tools can be divided into three groups: drawing tools, editing tools, and the text tool. The following table briefly describes the purpose of each tool and identifies its group.

Tool	Function
Scissors	(EDITING) Used to define a free-form area of a drawing. The defined area (referred to as a cutout) is enclosed within a dashed line.
Pick	(EDITING) Used to define a rectangular area of a drawing. The defined area (the cutout) is enclosed within a dashed line.
Airbrush	(DRAWING) Spray-paints an image of dots (with the foreground color) corresponding to the movements of the mouse.

Tool	Function
Text	(TEXT) Used for inserting text into drawings. Allows for the selection from available character fonts, sizes, and styles.
Color Eraser	(EDITING) Changes (erases) the selected foreground color to the background color as the cursor is dragged across the drawing area.
Eraser	(EDITING) Changes (erases) all colors to the background color as the cursor is dragged across the drawing area.
Paint Roller	(DRAWING) Fills an enclosed area with the foreground color.
Brush	(DRAWING) Used to create free-form lines and images.
Curve	(DRAWING) Used to create smooth curved lines.
Line	(DRAWING) Used to create straight lines.
Box	(DRAWING) Used to create empty rectangles.
Filled Box	(DRAWING) Used to create rectangles which display the foreground color inside the box and the background color surrounding the box.
Rounded Box	(DRAWING) Used to create empty rounded-corner rectangles.
Filled Rounded Box	(DRAWING) Used to create rounded-corner rectangles which display the foreground color inside the box and the background color surrounding the box.
Circle/Ellipse	(DRAWING) Used to create empty circles or ellipses.
Filled Circle/Ellipse	(DRAWING) Used to create circles or ellipses that display the foreground color inside the image and the background color surrounding the image.
Polygon	(DRAWING) Used to create a shape from a series of connected straight-line segments.
Filled Polygon	(DRAWING) Used to create a polygon filled with the foreground color and surrounded by the background color.

The Linesize Box

Located below the Toolbox is the Linesize box, which displays various line widths (see Figure 8.1). Use the Linesize box to set the line width for any of the drawing or editing tools being used to complete your drawing. To change line widths:

1. Move the pointer inside the Linesize box. (Once inside the Linesize box the pointer changes to a left pointing arrow.)

2. Position the pointer on the desired line width and click the mouse button.

   After you click on one of the line widths, the Linesize indicator arrow will point to your choice.

The Palette and the Foreground/Background Indicator

The Palette (see Figure 8.1), is located along the bottom of the Paintbrush window. It displays the choices of colors, or black-and-white patterns, to be used when creating the drawing. To switch from one mode to the other, choose the OPTIONS-Image Attributes... command to display the Image Attributes dialog box. Then select the corresponding option button in the Colors box. (Once a drawing is started, you may not switch modes.)

   The Foreground and Background indicators are located between the Palette and the Linesize Box (see Figure 8.1). The foreground Palette choice is shown as the inner box. The background choice is shown as the outer box. To change the foreground color or pattern, click on the desired choice with the *left* mouse button. To change the background color or pattern, click on the desired choice with the *right* mouse button.

Creating a Drawing

The basic steps for creating a drawing include:

- Selecting the desired tool.
- Selecting the line width.
- Selecting the foreground color.
- Selecting the background color.
- Creating the illustration.
- Editing the illustration.

Selecting a Tool

You select a tool by clicking on it. The background of the selected tool icon appears in a different color (or pattern) than the background of the other tool icons.

To use the selected tool:

1. Move the cursor to the desired starting position inside the drawing area.

2. Depress the mouse button and move the mouse in the manner corresponding with the image you are attempting to create.

3. When the image (or the desired portion of the image) has been drawn, release the button.

NOTE: Although you may not be able to create the exact images on the screen that you have pictured in your mind, remember, you do not need to be an artist to use Paintbrush. As you practice using the various Paintbrush tools, you may be surprised at the quality of the images you can create.

In the exercise below, you will briefly experiment with the Brush tool, various line widths, and the Palette. When you finish the steps, your window may look similar to Figure 8.3. (As you can see, the first exercise is very basic. As you move through the chapter, you will learn to use the tools to create more complex drawings.)

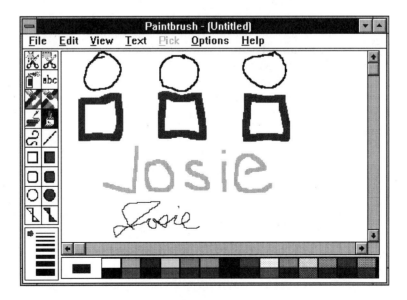

Figure 8.3 Sample results of the following exercise.

1. With the Paintbrush window open and the Brush tool selected, move the cursor about one-half inch inside the upper-left corner of the drawing area. Depress the mouse button and draw a circle with (approximately) a one-inch diameter; then release the button.

    Don't be concerned with drawing a "perfect" circle; you'll learn how to do that later. However, it is important that you draw a complete circle.

2. Draw two more similar circles along the top of the drawing area.

3. Select the thickest line in the Linesize box. Then move to the Palette and select a different foreground color. (Use the left mouse button to select the new color.)

4. Below each circle, draw a square with (about) one-inch sides (as in Figure 8.3).

5. Choose a "medium" line width from the Linesize box and a new foreground color from the Palette. Then *print* your first name below the squares. (Save at least one inch along the bottom of the drawing area for the next step.)

6. Choose a thin line and another foreground color. *Write* your first name in the space remaining near the bottom of the drawing area.

    Most likely, your window is fairly full. You may reveal more unoccupied space by manipulating the scroll bars and window borders. However, at this point we will use the FILE menu to save the file and clear the window.

The FILE Menu

The Paintbrush FILE menu includes the familiar New, Open..., Save, Save As..., Page Setup..., Print..., Print Setup..., and Exit commands you used with the previous accessories.

In the exercise below, you will use the *File Manager* to format the extra disk you previously used in Chapter 5 and then use the *Paintbrush* FILE menu to save the drawing you just created.

1. Minimize the Paintbrush window and note the Paintbrush icon at the bottom of the desktop. Display the Main window inside the Program Manager, then double-click on the File Manager icon to start the File Manager program.

2. Place the extra disk from Chapter 5 in the appropriate disk drive and use File Manager to format it. When the Format dialog box appears, choose the appropriate drive and storage capacity, and create a CH8 label for the disk.

3. After you have formatted your disk, minimize the File Manager and restore the Paintbrush window.

4 | Choose the FILE-Save As... command to display the Save As dialog box. Select the drive containing your CH8 disk. Then save your file as DRAW1 (let Paintbrush add its associated extension of BMP to the file name).

NOTE: As the file is being saved to your disk, the hour glass icon is displayed on your desktop. Once the file is saved, the hour glass is removed. Simple illustrations can occupy an enormous amount of storage space. This is why it may seem to take a long time for your file to be saved to your disk. (It also takes a longer time to save files to a floppy drive than to a hard drive or network drive.)

Once your file is saved, its name appears in the Paintbrush title bar.

5 | Choose the FILE-New command to display a clear drawing area.

TIP: When you create a fresh drawing area, the background color will remain the same as the background color of the previous drawing area. Before starting any exercise in this chapter, make sure that a white background has been selected.

NOTE: In the exercise above, you saved a drawing and then cleared the drawing area. To clear the drawing area without saving your drawing, choose the FILE-New command, or double-click on the Eraser tool.

Drawing Tools

It's time to experiment with some of the other drawing tools. In the following exercise you will use the Airbrush, Paint Roller, and Box tools, along with the EDIT-Undo command. When you finish steps 1–11 of the exercise, your window may look similar to the one in Figure 8.4.

1 | Load the DRAW1.BMP file. Select the Airbrush tool and the thickest line width. Then choose a light foreground color or pattern.

2 | Start in the middle of the window and "spray" a widening circle of dots on top of your drawing by depressing the mouse button and dragging the mouse in a widening circular motion. Vary the speed of the circular movement to see that as you slow your movements, you create a denser pattern of dots.

TIP: The width of the dot pattern corresponds to the selected line width.

3 | To remove the dots you just placed on your drawing, choose the EDIT-Undo command. The EDIT-Undo command removes all the work done on the drawing *since the last tool was selected*. Or, as in this case of selecting only one

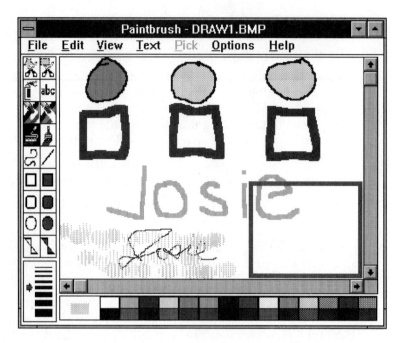

Figure 8.4 Sample results of completing steps 1–11.

tool since the file was opened, the EDIT-Undo command returns you to the original drawing.

4 | Look at the circles you drew at the top of the drawing area. If some of the circles are not complete, select the Brush tool to create a fully-enclosed circle.

NOTE: In the following step you will use the Paint Roller tool. The function of the Paint Roller is to cover the inside of a selected area with the color displayed in the Foreground Indicator. Two very important notes to remember when working with the Paint Roller are:

1. Make sure the shape you select is totally enclosed. If the outline of the shape has any openings, the entire surrounding area, not just the designated shape, will change to the selected foreground color or pattern when the mouse button is clicked (as the color "spills" out of its enclosure).

2. Make sure the lower-left *tip* of the Paint Roller cursor is placed in the area to be filled.

5 | Select the Paint Roller and a new foreground color. After positioning the lower left tip of the Paint Roller cursor in the left circle, click once. This causes the inside of the circle to be filled with the foreground color. Once the Paint Roller cursor is located inside any enclosed area and the mouse is clicked, the enclosed area is filled with the foreground color.

6 Choose another foreground color and use the Paint Roller to paint the inside of the remaining circles.

7 Select the (empty) Box tool and a medium line width.

NOTE: The procedure described below for using the empty Box tool may also be used for creating shapes with the (empty or filled) Box, Rounded Box, and Circle/Ellipse tools:

1. Select the appropriate tool and line width (line width determines the thickness of the shape's border).

2. Select the desired color(s). When creating *empty* shapes, the foreground color determines the color of the shape's border. When creating *filled* shapes, the foreground color is placed inside the shape and the background color is used to create the shape's border.

3. Position the cursor in the desired starting location (most people tend to initially position the cursor near the upper-left part of the shape and then draw diagonally downward toward the lower-right portion of the shape).

4. Depress the left mouse button and drag the mouse in a diagonal pattern. As you move the mouse, you change the shape of the box.

5. Release the mouse button after you are satisfied with the outline of the form.

8 Using the information above, create an empty box that starts near the center of the drawing area and extends to the lower-right corner of the drawing area. Most likely, the box will be placed over some of the letters in your name.

9 Remove the box by choosing the EDIT-Undo command. Note that the box is removed, but the circles that were filled with the Paint Roller still appear painted.

10 Draw another box in the lower-right corner of the drawing area.

11 Choose a light foreground color, then choose the Airbrush. Spray a light pattern of dots over the area where you wrote your first name. (After you complete this step, your window may look similar to Figure 8.4.)

12 Choose the FILE-New command. Because you are not saving the changes you just made, choose No when you receive the warning about saving your changes.

Straight Lines and Curved Lines

There are times when "almost straight" lines won't do. Fortunately, Paintbrush provides the means for creating perfectly straight vertical, horizontal, and diagonal lines. In addition, Paintbrush also provides a way to create smoothly curved lines.

Complete the following exercise to learn how to use the Brush tool to create straight vertical and horizontal lines. When you finish this exercise, your window may look similar to the one in Figure 8.5.

1 Start with a clear drawing area, a black foreground color and a white background color.

2 Select the Brush tool and the thinnest line width. Quickly draw two reasonably straight vertical lines that split the window into thirds.

3 Quickly draw a horizontal line across the center of your drawing area.

4 Select a new foreground color (i.e., red) and the next thicker line width.

5 Paintbrush provides numerous ways for drawing straight lines. One method involves holding down the Shift key, while using the Brush to create your lines.

   a. Place the cursor just to the right of the first vertical line created in step 2.

   b. Hold down the Shift key, then depress the mouse button and drag the cursor toward the bottom of the drawing area.

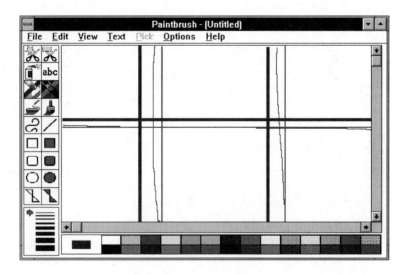

Figure 8.5 Sample results of the exercise above.

NOTE:

1. Don't be surprised to see your cursor moving slightly away from the straight line being drawn toward the bottom of the drawing area—the straight line is being drawn by the computer, whereas the position of the cursor corresponds to your mouse movements.

2. If you first moved the mouse in a horizontal direction, you will not be able to draw a vertical line until you release the Shift key and start over again. You'll learn how to erase images very soon, so if this happened, just start again.

c. When you reach the bottom of the drawing area, release the mouse button, then release the Shift key. This should have created a straight vertical line. Don't be concerned if your new line overlaps the previous line.

d. Repeat the above procedure to the right of the second vertical line.

e. Draw a straight horizontal line, just below the existing horizontal line, by following steps similar to the ones used for drawing straight vertical lines.

6. Choose a new color and a medium line width. Using the techniques discussed above, draw another set of straight lines on the opposite side of the original (somewhat crooked) lines you first created.

NOTE: Depressing the Shift key, while using the Brush tool, allows you to create *only* straight vertical and horizontal lines.

The *Line* tool, like the Brush, produces a line according to how the cursor was moved. The Brush tool leaves a path showing the exact route the cursor has traveled (hence the crooked line). When using the Line tool to draw a line, equal sections of the line (the straighter you move the mouse, the larger the line segments) are displayed in the drawing area. As long as you keep the mouse button depressed when using the Line tool, you can eventually position all the segments into one straight vertical, horizontal, or diagonal line.

A quick way to draw straight vertical, horizontal, or diagonal lines with the Line tool is to:

1. Depress the Shift key before depressing the mouse button.

2. Depress the mouse button and draw the desired line.

3. Release the mouse button, then release the Shift key.

Sometimes you may need to placed curved lines in your drawing. The steps for creating a curved line are listed below:

1. Select the Curve tool.

2. Draw a straight line and release the mouse button.

3. Move the cursor to the side of the line where the curve is to be placed.

4. Depress the mouse button and drag the cursor in the direction that you want the line to curve.

5. When the line is properly curved, release the mouse button.

If you want only one curve in the line, click on the second end point of the line. You may place a second curve in the line (in the opposite direction) by depressing the mouse button again and dragging the cursor away from the first curve. When the line is properly curved, release the button.

TIP: Before clicking on the second end point, or releasing the mouse button after making the second curve, you may undo a curve by clicking on the right mouse button.

The following exercise combines techniques you have previously used with instructions for using some new Paintbrush tools. The new tools you will work with include the Curve tool and the Pick tool. (The Pick tool is used for creating a *cutout* of a portion of the drawing you created. The exercise includes the instructions for using the Pick tool.) In this exercise you will draw two bananas. After finishing step 10, your results may look similar to Figure 8.6.

1 Make sure you have selected a black foreground and white background, then clear the drawing area without saving your changes. Reduce the size of the

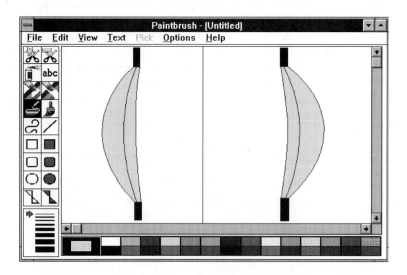

Figure 8.6 Sample results of the following exercise.

Paintbrush window so that at least one inch of the desktop appears on each side of the Paintbrush window.

2 Use the line tool to draw a straight vertical line down the center of your drawing area to create a left and right side.

(Steps 3–9 all take place in the left section of the drawing area.)

3 Choose the Filled Box tool, a black foreground *and* a black background. Then draw two thin (about ¼ inch by ½ inch) filled rectangles to serve as the top and bottom of a banana.

4 Choose a thin line width and the Curve tool. Then change the background color to white.

5 Draw the left side of the banana by drawing a line connecting the left sides of the two black rectangles.

6 Insert a curve in the line by moving the cursor to the left of the line (about half-way down), depressing the mouse button, and dragging the cursor to the left. As you drag the mouse, you see the line curve.

Because you want just a single curve, click on the end point of the line when you are satisfied with the shape of the curve.

7 Continue using the Curve tool to draw a line connecting the centers of the top and bottom of the banana. Curve this line to correspond with the first curve.

8 Continue using the Curve tool to connect the right side of the top and bottom of the banana. Curve this line to correspond with the previous two lines.

9 Choose a yellow foreground color and the Paint Roller tool to paint the two sections of the banana yellow.

10 In the right section of the drawing area, repeat steps 3–9 to create another banana that curves to the right. (Later in this chapter you will learn the commands for copying a drawing and flipping it vertically or horizontally and change its size.) When you finish this step your window should appear similar to the one in Figure 8.6.

NOTE: The Pick tool is used to draw a dashed rectangle around a particular portion of your drawing. After the desired items are enclosed within the dashed rectangle, they may be cut or copied to the Clipboard or saved to your disk—the portion of the drawing that has been placed within the rectangle is referred to as a *cutout*. In the steps below, you will create a cutout of the right banana and save a copy of it to your disk.

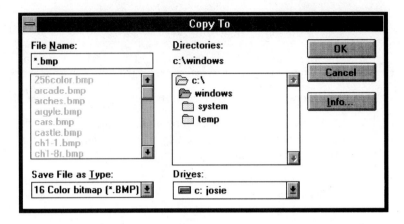

Figure 8.7 The Copy To dialog box.

11 Select the Pick tool (located in the upper-right corner of the Toolbox), and then use the same technique that you used with the Box tool to enclose the banana on the right side of the drawing area within the Pick tool's dashed rectangle.

12 Choose the EDIT-Copy To... command to display the Copy To dialog box shown in Figure 8.7. Enter the name BANANA in the File Name text box. If necessary choose the appropriate drive so that the cutout is saved to your CH8 disk, then press Enter or choose OK. (Let Paintbrush add its .BMP extension to your filename.)

13 Clear the present drawing from your Paintbrush window without saving the changes, and then load the BANANA.BMP file to see that you have saved a portion of your previous drawing. Then, minimize the Paintbrush window and open the File Manager window.

14 Display the directory contents of your CH8 disk and note the difference in byte size between saving an entire drawing, and saving a part of a drawing. (The byte size of the BANANA.BMP file is probably much smaller than the size of your DRAW1.BMP file. The smaller byte size and the ability to place cutouts in any number of drawings are two reasons why many users prefer to store Paintbrush cutouts instead of entire files on their disks.)

15 Close the File Manager window and restore the Paintbrush window. Then clear the Paintbrush window without saving your drawing.

Perfect Squares and Circles

To make perfect empty or filled squares, rounded squares, or circles:

1. Select the desired tool, foreground and background colors, and line width.

2. Depress the Shift key.

3. Depress the mouse button and create the desired shape.

4. Release the mouse button.

5. Release the Shift key.

Adding Text to an Image

Pictures may be worth a thousand words. However, adding a title, label, or other short pieces of text will often help the reader better understand your illustration. The Toolbox Text tool allows you to add text to your drawings.

Working with the Text tool consists of the following steps:

1. Select the Text tool. (The cursor will change to an I-beam once it enters the drawing area.)

2. (If desired) select a new foreground color for the text.

3. (If desired) choose the TEXT-Fonts... command to display the Font dialog box. Then make the desired selections from the font, style, and size boxes in the dialog box. You may also choose various character styles from the TEXT menu.

4. Move the I-beam to the desired location and click to place an insertion point at that location.

5. Enter the text.

Editing the Drawing

The editing tools include the color eraser, eraser, scissors, and pick.

The Color Eraser

The Color Eraser replaces the selected foreground color with the background color. There are two methods for using the Color Eraser. The first method involves working in a specific area of a drawing:

1. Select the Color Eraser.

2. Select the desired foreground and background colors.

3. Select the line width. (The wider the line, the wider the square eraser cursor becomes. Use a wide width for large-scale erasing. Use a narrower width for detailed erasing.)

4. Press the mouse button and drag the Color Eraser cursor over the particular area in the drawing where you want to change the selected foreground color to the selected background color.

5. Release the mouse button when you are finished.

A second way to use the Color Eraser is to replace all occurrences of one color with another. To use the second method:

1. Select the desired foreground and background colors.

2. Double-click on the Color Eraser icon.

Practice using the Color Eraser by completing the following exercise. When you have completed steps 1–5, your window may look similar to the one in Figure 8.8.

1   Start with a clear drawing area, a black foreground and a white background. Then create the largest empty perfect circle you can fit into your drawing area.

2   Choose a yellow foreground color, then use the Paint Roller tool to paint the inside of the circle yellow.

3   Using the text tool and your choice of font, place the numbers 12, 3, 6, and 9 around the circle so that the circle appears as a clock face.

4   Click on the center of the clock, then choose a red foreground color, a medium line width, and the Line tool to set the time of your clock to 3:00.

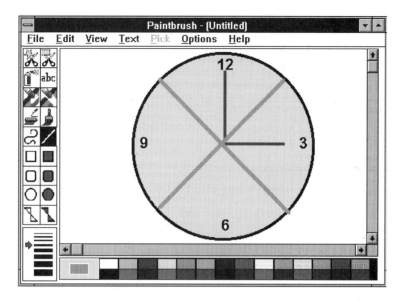

Figure 8.8 Results of completing steps 1–5.

5 Choose a green foreground color and use the Line tool to create two diagonal lines forming a green X over the face of the clock.

6 Select a light gray background color.

7 Select the Color Eraser.

8 When you move the Color Eraser cursor—a box displaying a large "+" symbol inside—into the drawing area, you see that the eraser is much larger than the selected line width. If you like, you may select a line width that more closely corresponds with the width of the lines in the X. (In this case a larger eraser actually makes the erasing easier.)

9 Drag the cursor over the lines in the X to see the X become the same color as the selected background color.

10 Select a light gray foreground color and a yellow background color that matches the background color of the clock.

11 Move the cursor over the X again. This time the X should be erased into the background.

NOTE: Depending on the colors used to create items in your drawings, this technique may modify the colors or erase parts of the foreground items. (In the previous step, if your X extended into the border of the circle, some of the border may have been changed to the background color of the clock face. Step 11 may also have caused parts of the lines, used for the clock hands, to be erased.) This is not important for this exercise, but it is important to remember that the Color Eraser should be carefully used when editing.

12 To see how you can just double-click on the icon of the Color Eraser tool to change the foreground color to the background color, complete the following steps.

a. Reselect the red color used to create the clock hands as the foreground color.

b. Select a blue background color.

c. Move to the Toolbox and double-click on Color Eraser. (This causes all occurrences of the foreground color to change to the background color.)

13 Keep your drawing on your desktop and move to the next section.

The Eraser

When you drag the Eraser cursor, you paint the background color over all items in the Eraser's path. Whereas the Color Eraser is designed to remove one color, the Eraser removes the entire image.

Using the drawing from the previous exercise, practice using the Eraser by completing the steps below.

1 Select the Eraser tool, a medium line width, and a white background color.

2 Erase the lower half of the clock face by moving the cursor back and forth underneath the 9 and the 3 on the clock face.

3 Choose a brown background color and erase most of the clock face.

4 Double-click on the Eraser icon to tell Windows to load a fresh drawing area. Do not save your changes.

5 Notice that your new drawing area has a brown background. Change the background to white and double-click the eraser again—this should display a new drawing area with a white background.

The Scissors

The Scissors tool, like the Pick tool, is used to define a cutout. You have already used the Pick tool to create a *rectangular* cutout of a drawing, which was then saved as the BANANA.BMP file. The Scissors tool allows you to make a cutout of an *irregularly shaped area* of your drawing. For example, using the Scissors tool would have enabled you to make a cutout that closely followed the curves in the shape of the banana in the BANANA.BMP file. Whenever you create a cutout, you automatically activate the PICK menu. (This menu is discussed in the following section.)

You may use the EDIT menu and the Clipboard to cut, copy, and paste cutouts created with the Scissors or Pick tool. However, in the following exercise you will use the Scissors tool to create cutouts and then learn to move and copy the cutouts into different locations in the same drawing *without* going through the intermediate step of storing the images on the Clipboard and then transferring them back to your drawing.

1 Start with a clear drawing area, a black foreground color, and a white background color. Use the Line tool to divide your drawing area into four quarters. After forming the four sections, use the Text tool to label the top two sections 1 and 2, and the bottom two sections 3 and 4.

NOTE: After entering the last number, reposition the cursor into the first section. If you don't reposition the cursor, when you complete step 2 you will inadvertently change the color of the last number you entered.

2 Change the foreground color to yellow and the background color to gray. Choose a medium line width, and then choose the Filled Circle/Ellipse tool and create a perfect filled circle in section 1 (the upper-left section).

3 Change the background color to white. (If you omit this step, you will only be able to reposition the inside of the circle as you complete the next steps.)

4 Choose the Scissors tool and then create a cutout of the image in section 1 by following the steps below:

a. Move the cursor to the desired starting point.

b. Depress the mouse button and carefully enclose the image. (If you get close to completing your loop, you may release the mouse button and have Paintbrush draw a straight line from your current position to your starting position and thus, complete the loop for you.)

c. Release the mouse button.

TIP: If you make a mistake while creating your cutout, either click the right mouse button, or release the mouse button, move the cursor away from the cutout, and click the left mouse button to clear the cutout.

5 Copy the image in the cutout into section 2 by following the steps below:

a. Place the cursor inside the cutout.

b. Depress the Ctrl key, then depress the left mouse button.

c. Drag a copy of the image into section 2 of your drawing, release the Ctrl key, and then release the mouse button.

d. Click outside the cutout to anchor it in place.

6 In this step you will *move* the image from section 1 to section 4.

a. Create a new cutout of the circle in section 1.

b. Place the cursor inside the cutout.

c. Depress the left mouse button.

d. Drag the image into section 4 of your drawing and then release the mouse button. THEN LEAVE THE CURSOR INSIDE THE CUTOUT and complete the next step.

7 Currently your circle is located in sections 2 and 4, and the cutout still appears in section 4. (If the circle in section 4 is no longer enclosed in the cutout, create a new cutout in section 4.) Copy the same circle into sections 1 and 3 by following the steps below:

a. Depress the Ctrl key, then depress the left mouse button.

b. Drag a copy of the image into section 3 of your drawing and release the mouse button, keeping the Ctrl Button depressed.

c. Depress the mouse button again and (with the Ctrl key still depressed) drag the image into section 1.

d. Release the Ctrl key, release the mouse button, and then click outside of the cutout to lock in the image in section 1. (When you finish this step you should have an identical circle placed in all four sections.)

TIP: As you just saw, by keeping the Ctrl key depressed throughout the copy procedure, you may copy the same image as many times as needed.

NOTE: The easiest way to see what happens if you drag an object to a new location, while the background indicator is not the same color as the background of the drawing area, is to repeat the exercise omitting step 3. (You will see that all the area within the cutout will move; however, once the cutout is moved, that portion of the drawing area is displayed in the current background color. When changing background colors and moving cutouts, it is easy to inadvertently change your drawing in ways you may not have anticipated.)

8 Clear the drawing area without saving your changes, and then repeat all the above steps, except step 3, and notice how your drawing is affected.

The PICK Menu

Once a cutout is created (through the use of the Pick or the Scissors tool), the PICK menu is activated. The menu remains dimmed when no cutout exists in the current drawing. The commands available in the PICK menu are listed below.

Commands	Function
Flip Horizontal	turns the cutout from side to side
Flip Vertical	turns the cutout upside-down
Inverse	displays the complementary cutout colors
Shrink + Grow	allows for adjusting the size of the cutout
Tilt	allows for displaying the cutout at an angle
Clear	changes the original cutout to the selected background when the Tilt or Shrink + Grow command is used

With a little experimentation and practice, you will quickly learn how to use the PICK menu to give the same cutout many different appearances.

Changing the Paintbrush Window

The VIEW menu provides commands to alter the appearance of the Paintbrush window. The commands of the VIEW menu are listed below.

Command	Function
Zoom In	Enlarges one part of the drawing so that it may be edited one pixel at a time. Also returns a drawing to standard size after the Zoom Out command has been chosen.
Zoom Out	Displays the whole drawing when the normal-size drawing does not fit in the window. Also returns the drawing to standard size after the Zoom In command has been chosen.

Command	Function
View Picture	Displays only the drawing (what you will see when the drawing is printed).
Tools and Linesize	Command that toggles between removing and displaying the Toolbox and Linesize box in the window.
Palette	Command that toggles between removing and displaying the Palette and the Foreground/Background Indicator in the window.
Cursor Position	Displays a dialog box showing the x and y coordinates of the current cursor position.

Zooming In and Zooming Out

The Zoom In/Zoom Out command sequence allows you to draw a small rectangular image, pixel by pixel, and then return to the standard-size drawing. This sequence gives you the most control over the details in your drawing. Complete the following exercise to learn how to use the VIEW-Zoom In command. When you finish the first 5 steps, your window may resemble the one shown in Figure 8.9.

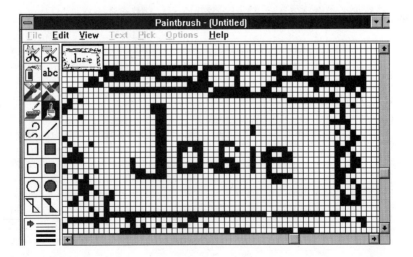

Figure 8.9 Sample results of steps 1–5.

1. Start with a clear drawing area, a black foreground, and a white background. Then choose the Brush tool.

2. Choose the VIEW-Zoom In command to display a small rectangle in the drawing area.

3. Move the rectangle (by moving the mouse WITHOUT depressing a button) to the upper-right corner of the drawing area. (For future reference, note that the rectangle can be moved to any location within the drawing area.) Once the box is in the desired location, click the left mouse button to secure the location. This step changes the drawing area to a grid pattern to illustrate each pixel.

4. Enter your first name in the grid by either clicking on each of the appropriate squares, or by keeping the mouse button depressed and dragging the cursor over the squares to be painted in the foreground color.

   The actual image that will be displayed in the drawing area is shown in the box in the upper-left corner of the drawing area.

TIP: For solid-color shapes, once you create the enclosed frame with the Brush tool (for example, a tall, thin rectangle for the letter "I"), use the Paint Roller to paint the inside of the shape with one click of the mouse.

5. After entering your name, draw a border around it.

TIP: If a square was accidently painted, return it to the background color by placing the cursor on the square and clicking the right mouse button.

6. Choose the VIEW-Zoom Out command to return to the normal view of the drawing area and note your name in the upper-right corner of the drawing area.

7. Keep your drawing on the desktop and move to the next section.

Displaying More Drawing Space

You already know that one way to display more drawing space is to maximize the Paintbrush window on your desktop. Complete the following exercise to practice using other commands for displaying additional drawing space. (For the steps below, use the same drawing you completed in the previous exercise.)

1. Currently your name appears in the upper-right corner of the drawing area; make a copy of this image and place it in the lower-right corner of the drawing area.

2. Manipulate the vertical and horizontal scroll bars to view the additional drawing area not displayed through the current window.

3 Return each scroll box to the beginning of its scroll bar.

4 Removing the Toolbox and Linesize box creates a wider drawing area and still allows you to use the selected tool and line width. Complete the following steps to remove, and then return, the Toolbox and Linesize box:

   a. Choose the VIEW-Tools and Linesize command to remove the Toolbox and Linesize box.

   b. Once the items are removed from the window, choose the VIEW-Tools and Linesize box command again to return the items to the window.

5 Removing the Palette and Foreground and Background Indicators creates a longer drawing area and still allows you to use the selected colors. Complete the following steps to remove, and then return, the Palette and Foreground/Background Indicators:

   a. Choose the VIEW-Palette command to remove the Palette and Foreground/Background Indicators.

   b. Once the items are removed from the window, choose the VIEW-Palette command again to re-display the Palette and Foreground/Background Indicators.

If you use one of the above techniques to create a drawing that is larger than can be displayed within the normal Paintbrush window, you can still view the total results of your work by choosing either the VIEW-Picture command or the VIEW-Zoom Out command.

If you choose the VIEW-Picture command, your entire desktop becomes the drawing area. You may view your entire picture, but you may not edit the picture in this mode. To return the Paintbrush window to the screen, just click the mouse button.

Choosing the VIEW-Zoom Out command reduces your drawing so that it fits within your current window. This command is most useful when you need to create (or insert) a cutout that is too large to appear in any other type of Paintbrush window. The only editing that can be done in this mode is through the EDIT menu.

Fine-Tuning the Cursor Position

To set the exact location of the cursor, use the VIEW-Cursor Position command. By knowing exactly where you want the cursor to be placed, you may return to a specific point in your drawing to complete any editing, or place a cutout precisely at the desired location.

The cursor location is specified by identifying its vertical and horizontal position in relationship to the upper-left corner of the drawing area. Concepts used to specify the cursor location include:

- Two coordinates (x and y) are used to pinpoint the cursor location. The x coordinate relates to horizontal placement of the cursor; the y coordinate relates to vertical placement.

- The upper-left corner of the drawing area is position 0, 0.

To fine-tune the position of the cursor, follow the steps below:

1. Determine the desired x and y coordinates.

2. Choose the VIEW-Cursor Position command to display a dialog box listing the current x and y coordinates of the cursor (this box appears near the sizing buttons in the Paintbrush window). These coordinates change as the cursor is moved.

3. After using the mouse to move the cursor close to the desired coordinates, use the up, down, left and right cursor control keyboard keys to move the cursor one pixel at a time to the exact desired location.

To turn the Cursor Position dialog box off, double-click on its Control-menu box or select the VIEW-Cursor Position command again.

Printing a Drawing

Choosing the FILE-Print... command displays the Print dialog box (see Figure 8.10).

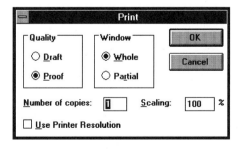

Figure 8.10 The Print dialog box.

The options for the Print dialog box are explained below.

Option	Purpose
Quality	
Draft	Creates a lower-quality printout than the Proof quality. Depending on the printer, selecting this option may speed the printing process.
Proof	Higher-quality (more dots per inch) printout. Allows for the use of printer's advanced features. (This is the default Quality setting).
Window	
Whole	Prints entire drawing, including parts not appearing in the drawing area on the screen. (This is the default Window setting).
Partial	Prints part of the drawing. User must select desired area of drawing to print.
Number of Copies	Sets number of copies to be printed.
Scaling	Allows for increasing or decreasing the size of the printed image. (The number 100 indicates no scaling. Enter a number less than 100 to make the image smaller; to make it larger, enter a number greater than 100.)
Use Printer Resolution	By default Paintbrush prints at the screen's resolution. Printer resolutions often provide a smaller image because the printer dots are usually smaller than the monitor dots. Choosing this option usually produces a smaller printed output. For additional sizing alternatives, use the Scaling option described above.

To print a drawing:

1. Make sure the printer is ready, then choose the FILE-Print... command to display the Print dialog box.

2. Enter the desired options and values in the dialog box.

3. Click on OK, or press Enter, to start the printer.

TIP: When using a single-color printer to print a multi-colored drawing, you may be somewhat surprised at how some colors are represented in your printout. To have the best idea of how the printed output will appear when a single-color printer is used, choose the OPTIONS-Image Attributes... command to display the Image Attributes dialog box, then choose the Black and White Color option BEFORE beginning your drawing.

Summary

The purpose of this chapter was to provide an introduction to the **Paintbrush accessory**. Along with the standard window elements, the Paintbrush window includes the Drawing Area (defined as the work area in other windows), Toolbox, Linesize Box, Foreground/Background Indicator, and the Palette. Use of a pointing device, such as a mouse, is essential to fully utilize the options presented in the Paintbrush accessory.

The **Paintbrush Toolbox** consists of many tools, including those that enable the user to place straight lines, curved lines, free-hand drawn lines, empty and filled boxes, empty and filled circles/ellipses, and empty and filled polygons into the drawing area. The Airbrush tool enables the user to "spray" a pattern of dots on the drawing area. The Paint Roller tool allows the user to "paint" the inside of an enclosed shape with the click of a mouse button. The Eraser lets the user erase an area of the painting and change the entire "erased" area to the selected background color. The Color Eraser enables the user to change the "erased" foreground color to the selected background color. Rectangular cutouts of sections of the drawing area may be created by using the Pick tool. The Scissors tool allows the user to create an irregular-shaped cutout.

The line width selected in the **Linesize Box** (located below the Toolbox) determines the width of the lines, or the borders of the shapes, that will next be entered into the drawing area. To select a particular width (from the eight widths available), move the pointer onto the desired width and click the mouse; a right arrow appears next to the selected width.

The **Foreground/Background Indicator** consists of two boxes located to the right of the Linesize Box. The inner box displays the foreground choice from the Palette; the outer box displays the background choice.

The **Palette,** located below the drawing area, consists of two rows of boxes displaying the colors (or black-and-white patterns) available to the user. The user chooses a foreground color (or pattern) by placing the pointer on the desired Palette choice and clicking the left mouse button. The foreground choice determines the color (or pattern) used for drawing lines or the interior of the filled boxes, circles/ellipses, or polygons. The user selects the background choice by placing the pointer on the desired Palette choice and clicking the right mouse button. The background color (or pattern) is used to show the borders of filled shapes; or, when erasing an item from the drawing area, the "erased" area is replaced with the current background color.

New menus discussed in this chapter included the PICK and VIEW menus. The **PICK menu** is activated after a cutout is created. The commands included in this menu allow the user to flip the cutout either vertically or horizontally, shrink or grow the image in the cutout, tilt the image in the cutout, or change the cutout's background when the Tilt or Shrink + Grow commands are used.

The **VIEW menu** enables the user to "Zoom In" on a small piece of the drawing area to work on part of a drawing, one pixel at a time. The VIEW menu includes the option to "Zoom Out" to either return to a normal mode after zooming in on a small area of the drawing area, or to view a painting that is too large to completely fit into the Paintbrush window. The **VIEW-View Picture** command removes all items, except the drawing, from the screen. Additional options of the VIEW menu allow for showing the cursor position as an x-y coordinate and removing (or restoring) the Toolbox, Linesize Box, Foreground/Background Indicator, and Palette from the Paintbrush window.

Two cautions to remember when using any painting program:

1. Set a realistic goal concerning the quality of your painting. Consider the purpose of the painting and the level of detail truly needed.

2. Set a realistic deadline for completing the painting. It is very easy to get overly involved in creating the images. Be sure to keep your time investment in the painting in perspective compared to the rest of the project.

Applications

1. Use Paintbrush to create a drawing by utilizing the following steps:

   a. Create a one-inch horizontal border along the top of the drawing area. Fill the border with the design of your choice.

   b. Copy the border to the bottom of the drawing area.

   c. Vertically flip the bottom border so that it mirrors the top border. (Hint: Use the PICK menu.)

   d. Create a one-inch border along the left side of the drawing area. Fill the border with the design of your choice.

e. Copy the left border to the right side.

f. Horizontally flip the right border so that it mirrors the left border.

g. Use at least four Paintbrush tools to create the drawing of your choice.

h. Print your drawing and identify, on the printout, where you used the various Paintbrush tools.

i. Use the scissors or pick tool to create a cutout of the drawing inside the borders.

j. Clear your Paintbrush window.

2. Using the Text tool and at least three other Paintbrush tools, create your own (8.5 × 11 inch) letterhead. Print one copy of your letterhead. Create a cutout of your letterhead and save it as APP8-2.BMP on your CH8 disk.

9

Transferring Information Among Applications

In Chapter 7 you used the Windows Clipboard to transfer text between Write documents. In this chapter you will explore additional ways to transfer information between applications as you learn to:

1. copy an image of the entire desktop into an application window.

2. copy the image of the active window from the desktop into an application window.

3. move and size Paintbrush images inserted into Write documents.

4. explore the benefits of object linking and embedding (OLE).

Copying an Image of the Desktop into a Window

In your previous work with the Clipboard and the Write accessory, you learned to transfer text among documents. Along with transferring text, you may occasionally find a need to capture an image of your desktop and place that image into a document.

To copy an image of the entire desktop into an application window:

1. Press the Print Scrn key to place an image of the desktop onto the Clipboard.

2. Place the cursor in the appropriate location in the desired Windows application window and choose EDIT-Paste.

Copying an Image of the Active Window into a Window

To copy an image of the *active* window into another window:

1. Make the desired window active.

2. Press Alt+Print Scrn to place an image of the active window on the Clipboard.

3. Place the cursor in the appropriate location in the desired Windows application window and choose EDIT-Paste.

Placing a Non-Windows Application Inside a Window

Windows 3.1 may run in either the standard mode or the 386 enhanced mode. The standard mode is more restrictive but does not require as powerful computing hardware as the 386 enhanced mode. You cannot run a DOS application in a window when using Windows in the standard mode.

When running Windows in the 386 enhanced mode, it is possible to run a non-Windows (DOS) application inside a window. (See Appendix for more information.)

TIP: To verify the mode you are running in, open the HELP menu from an application window menu bar and choose the About command. Along with other information, the corresponding dialog box displays the current Windows mode.

To efficiently run a DOS program through Windows, a special program information file (PIF) may be created to help Windows manage the non-Windows software. Included in this PIF is the information that determines whether the DOS application initially appears in a window or in the full-screen mode when the program first appears on your screen. PIF's for the more common DOS programs, such as WordPerfect and Lotus 1-2-3, are already included in your Windows 3.1 package. For more information on PIF files and the Windows PIF Editor, refer to your Windows manuals.

When running in the 386 enhanced mode, if a DOS application initially occupies the entire screen, you may place it in a window by pressing Alt+Enter. The DOS application is placed in a window that includes sizing buttons, a title bar, a Control Menu box, and borders, but does not include a menu bar. The sizing buttons, title bar, and borders function in the same manner as in other windows. The Control menu for a DOS application window has some commands that are different from the commands on the Control menus in Windows applications.

NOTE: Although a DOS application may be placed within a window, it is still necessary to use the program's exit routine to end the program. You may not use a Windows command to close a DOS program window.

Copying Information from DOS Applications

To copy information from a DOS application window to the Clipboard:

1. Choose the Edit command from the DOS window's Control menu.

2. Choose the Mark command from the Edit submenu.

3. Select the desired information.

4. Choose the Edit command again from the Control menu.

5. Choose the Copy command from the Edit submenu.

To copy text from a DOS application running in the full screen mode into a Windows application:

1. Display the desired DOS application text.

2. Press the Print Scrn button.

3. Open the Windows application and position the insertion point in the desired location.

4. Choose the (Windows application's) EDIT-Paste command.

Inserting a Paintbrush Cutout into a Write Document

While it is useful to know how to transfer an image of your desktop or active window into a Windows application, in most cases, the information that you transfer will consist of placing information from part of one document into another document. The following exercise gives you a chance to combine text and graphics in the same document as you will place part of a Paintbrush file into a Write document. You will also learn to manipulate a graphic image inside the Write word processor.

1 Insert your CH8 disk (the one holding the files you created with the Paintbrush accessory in Chapter 8) into the appropriate drive. Display the contents of this disk inside a File Manager directory window. Double-click on the DRAW1.BMP file name to launch the Paintbrush program and display the DRAW1.BMP file. (Remember, this can be done because the BMP extension is associated with the Paintbrush program.)

2 Select the Scissors tool and create a cutout of your written name.

3 Choose the EDIT-Cut command to remove the cutout from the drawing and place it on the Clipboard. Then close the Paintbrush window without saving your changes.

4 Open the Write accessory and key your name and today's date along the top of the page. Then press Enter twice and enter the following text:

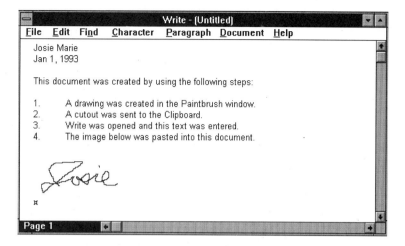

Figure 9.1 Sample results of completing steps 1–5.

This document was created by using the following steps:

1. A drawing was created in the Paintbrush window.
2. A cutout was sent to the Clipboard.
3. Write was opened and this text was entered.
4. The image below was pasted into this document.

5 Press Enter twice, then use the (Write) EDIT-Paste command to paste the cutout underneath step 4 of your Write document.

After you add the graphic image to your Write file, your document may look similar to the one in Figure 9.1.

6 Name this file PBWRITE1 and save it as a Write file on the CH8 disk (leave the file in the Write window).

7 Return to the document and select the area containing the illustration by placing the I-beam pointer on your signature and clicking the mouse button once. Then delete the signature (press the Delete key) and save this file as PBWRITE2, on the CH8 disk.

8 Open File Manager and compare the byte size of the PBWRITE1.WRI file (which includes your signature) and PBWRITE2.WRI (no image included) to see how many bytes are needed to save a simple illustration.

TIP: Many people prefer using high density (instead of double-density) floppy disks when saving files that include images because of the large amount of disk space required to store the images.

9 Close File Manager and return to the Write window. Load the PBWRITE1.WRI file and click once on your signature to select it.

NOTE: When you select an image inside a Write document, you activate a number of commands from the Write EDIT menu that were previously inactive.

10 Choose the EDIT-Move Picture command.

NOTE: Once this command is chosen, the image that appeared in reverse video (to show it was selected) appears in a normal mode. However, the image is surrounded by a light-colored rectangular frame. You may move this frame to the left or right by dragging the mouse WITHOUT depressing the mouse button. Once the frame is in the desired position, click the mouse to secure the cutout's new location.

11 Move the image to the center of your document and click the mouse once to secure the new location.

12 With the image still selected, choose the (Write) EDIT-Size Picture command.

NOTE: Once this command is chosen, a light-colored frame surrounds the selected image (which again appears in the normal mode). Move the mouse, WITHOUT depressing the mouse button, to re-size the frame to the desired dimensions for the image, then click the button to secure the new size for the image.

13 Re-size your image to appear wider and longer than the cutout you originally placed in the document, then click the mouse once to secure the new size.

14 Name this file PBWRITE3.WRI and save it on your CH8 disk. Then clear the Write window and move to the following section.

An Introduction to Object Linking and Embedding (OLE)

NOTE: The following terms are commonly used when working with object linking and embedding:

Compound Document: a document that was created from files, or parts of files, from two or more documents.

Object: either a copy of the data (text, graphic, sound, or video) from the source document in the server application, or a "pointer" to the data in the server application.

Server Application: the source application used to create the original data. (In Windows 3.1, the Paintbrush and the Sound Recorder are server applications.)

Client Application: the application that is receiving and storing the object. (In Windows 3.1, Write and Cardfile are client applications.)

Linking: placing an object in the client document that serves as a "pointer," or link, to the desired area of the source document (in the server application). Because linking uses the "pointer" concept, linking does not place a duplicate copy of the data from the source document into the client document.

Embedding: placing an object in the client document that contains a copy of the desired data from the source document. When using the embedding feature, data from one file becomes part of the file to which it is pasted.

As you completed the previous exercise, you were able to move and size the image; but what happens if you need to modify the picture in the text document? The Windows 3.1 *object linking and embedding* (OLE) feature makes it easy to create (and modify) a compound document. You may use the Clipboard and the commands from the EDIT menu to transfer the data from one document into another. When the compound document is open, OLE furnishes a convenient (two-way) pathway to and from the various source applications used in creating the pieces of the document. If editing is necessary in any part of a compound document (i.e., a Paintbrush image in a Write file needs to be updated), you need only to double-click on the desired information to recall the source application and load the data in the source application's work area. You then make your corrections using the original source application. Your choice of linking or embedding the information determines how the modifications are placed in the compound document.

Linking allows you to maintain one copy of "core information" that may be linked to many client documents. Then, if changes are made to the core information, OLE provides the means to quickly update all of the linked client documents. For example, if a map showing the location of your company's summer picnic was saved in a file created in Paintbrush, and that file was linked into 50 other files created with Write (possibly letters to your employees), when you update your map in the Paintbrush file (i.e., to change the picnic site), the change is automatically forwarded to all of the linked Write files.

The object being linked into a client application does not become part of the client file, but (through its relationship with the source program) the linked object appears in the display and will print with the client file. Linking is especially useful for data that is constantly being updated, since the other files draw from the source file to display the linked information.

If you were to take a copy of this compound document file to a meeting and the computer you plan to use (at the meeting) has access only to Write, you should embed (rather than link) the map into your Write document. An embedded object becomes part of the client document and no longer needs a relationship with the server application to be displayed or printed.

Not all programs can use OLE; those that can are referred to as OLE-supporting programs. The four OLE-supporting programs that come with Windows are Write, Cardfile, Sound Recorder, and Paintbrush. In the previous exercise, you created an image with the Paintbrush accessory and copied that image into a Write document. Because both Paintbrush and Write are OLE-supporting programs, you actually *embedded* the image into the Write document. (At this point you can enter either the PBWRITE1.WRI or BPWRITE3.WRI files to modify your signature without first completing the normal procedure for opening the Paintbrush window and loading the DRAW1.BMP file. If either Paintbrush or Write was not an OLE-supporting program, the pasted image would be static, which means you would not be able to modify it while it was inside of the Write document.)

After you become comfortable with the OLE concepts, you may want to learn how to use the Object Packager accessory. Using the Object Packager allows you to create packages (or icons) that represent objects and then insert the packages into the client documents. See your Windows Help facility and manuals for information on this useful accessory.

Complete the following exercise, using an OLE-server program (Paintbrush) and an OLE-client program (Write), to practice working with the *linking* aspect of OLE.

NOTE: There is a good possibility that, at some point in this exercise, you may receive a message that you have run out of storage space on your disk. If this happens, use the File Manager to delete any of the files previously saved on your CH8 disk (starting with DRAW1.BMP and BANANA.BMP).

1 Display the Write window on the right half of your desktop. Then open the Paintbrush window and size it to fill most of the left side of the desktop. Choose a black foreground and a white background. Move to the Paintbrush window and use the appropriate tools to create the map displayed in Figure 9.2.

2 In the Write window create the short memo displayed in Figure 9.3. After completing the RSVP line, press Enter twice.

3 Save the map as a Paintbrush file, called MAP.BMP on your CH8 disk. (Any data to be linked must be saved at least once in a file. This saved Paintbrush file contains information needed to complete the linking activity.)

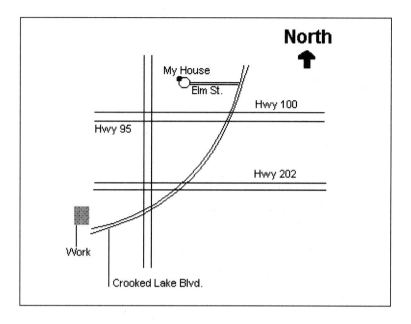

Figure 9.2 Map (created in Paintbrush) for the *linking* exercise.

4 Use the Pick tool to make a cutout of the map and copy it to the Clipboard by choosing the (Paintbrush) EDIT-Copy command.

5 Move to the Write window and choose the (Write) EDIT-Paste Link command. (This command places the map inside your Write document; a link has now been established between the two files.)

  Close the Paintbrush window and maximize the Write window to see how the map and the text appear together.

6 Save this Write file as BUD.WRI on your CH8 disk and leave the file displayed in the Write window.

7 In the Write window, change the TO: BUD section to read TO: ROGER MARKS. Then save the revised file as ROGER.WRI on your disk and keep the ROGER.WRI file displayed in the Write window. (This step creates a link between the MAP.BMP file and the ROGER.WRI files.)

8 To make the map a little more specific (and to demonstrate the linking feature), add a small lake to the right of Crooked Lake Blvd., between Hwys 100 and 202. Complete this procedure by following the steps below.

PARTY INVITATION

TO: Bud

FROM: Don

DATE: Jan 4

Please come to a party at my house (1223 Elm St.) starting at 8:00 pm this Friday.

I live 6 miles north of our company. See map below for directions.

RSVP my office.

Figure 9.3 Memo (created in Write) for the *linking* exercise.

a. Double-click on the map in the ROGER.WRI document. This causes Windows to launch the server application (Paintbrush) and load the MAP.BMP file in the work area. (This Paintbrush window will become the active window on your desktop.) Keep the map in the ROGER.WRI file visible on the desktop as you complete the remaining steps in the Paintbrush window.

b. In the Paintbrush window, use the empty Circle/Ellipse tool (keep the same black foreground and white background colors) to create a small lake at the location described above. As soon as you create the lake in the Paintbrush window, your edits are automatically linked into the ROGER.WRI file. (If you kept the map portion of the ROGER.WRI file displayed, you saw how quickly the lake was inserted).

c. Save your revised Paintbrush drawing (using the same name—MAP.BMP) and close the Paintbrush program.

d. In the Write window, save the revised ROGER.WRI file. Then open the BUD.WRI file. When you see the dialog box asking if you want to update the links now (see Figure 9.4) choose Yes.

This step may take a little while because the system is searching through files which are stored on your floppy disk. When the computer finishes its searching activities, an updated map is displayed in the BUD.WRI document.

As evidenced in the updated BUD.WRI file, when files share a common linked object, they do not have to be open while the linked object is being updated in the server application.

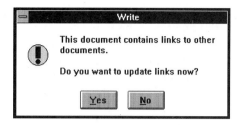

Figure 9.4 Confirmation dialog box for updating linked information.

This OLE exercise was designed to introduce you to the Windows OLE feature. More and more software programs are being written to take advantage of the Windows *object linking and embedding* feature. Depending on the applications you are using, the OLE feature may be one of the most useful and powerful Windows features you will use in your computing.

Summary

This chapter focused on various techniques for capturing information and then transferring it from one document into another.

To **send a picture of the desktop to the Clipboard,** press the Print Scrn button.

To **send a picture of the active window to the Clipboard,** press Alt+Print Scrn.

To **run a DOS application inside a window,** you must run Windows in the 386 enhanced mode. Once Windows is loaded, you may start the DOS application from either the Program Manager or the File Manager. If the DOS application is running in the full-screen mode, you may place the application inside a window by pressing Alt+Enter. The DOS application window appears similar to Windows application windows; however, the DOS application window does not include a menu bar.

A Paintbrush picture inserted into a Write document may be moved by choosing the (Write) **EDIT-Move Picture command.** Similarly, a Paintbrush picture inserted into a Write document may be sized by choosing the (Write) **EDIT-Size Picture** command.

Object Linking and Embedding (OLE) is a very important feature of Windows 3.1. The basic purpose of OLE is to provide a simple yet powerful method for sharing data between programs. An object is either a copy of the data (text, graphic, sound, or video) from the source document in the server application, or a "pointer" to the data in the server application. *Object linking* is placing an object in the client document that serves as a "pointer," or link to the desired area of the source document (in the server application). Because linking uses the "pointer" concept, linking does not place a duplicate copy of the data from the source document into the client document. *Embedding an object* consists of placing an object from the source document into the client document. When using the embedding feature, data from one file becomes part of the file to which it is pasted.

▬▬▬▬▬▬ Applications ▬▬▬▬▬▬

NOTE: If you run short of disk storage space before completing these Applications, remove any of the files on the CH8 disk except the MAP.BMP, BUD.WRI, and ROGER.WRI files.

1. a. In the introduction to Object Linking and Embedding section of this chapter, you wrote two invitations for a party you were hosting. To further help the people find your house, use the necessary Paintbrush tools to make a drawing of the front of your house (or draw the front of your dream house). Save the drawing as HOUSE.BMP and then link the drawing to the end of both invitations (the BUD.WRI and ROGER.WRI files). Save the revised BUD.WRI and ROGER.WRI files under their current names and leave the ROGER.WRI file on your desktop.

   b. Through the ROGER.WRI file, return to the Paintbrush window displaying the HOUSE.BMP file. Use the Paintbrush Text tool to display the phrase "My House" somewhere in your drawing. Then complete the necessary steps to see that both the BUD.WRI and ROGER.WRI files receive the updated drawing.

   c. Print one of the revised invitations.

2. For this application you are the owner of three different companies. Utilize the Cardfile accessory to create a three-card file where each card lists the name and address of one of the companies. Save this file as TYCOON.CRD.

   Use the Paintbrush accessory to create a separate logo for each company and *embed* the logo into the corresponding card. (Hint: You may need to look at the Cardfile Help facility to learn how to embed pictures into Cardfile files.) Resave the file as TYCOON.CRD and print your three cards.

10

The Control Panel

The Control Panel is the Windows module that enables you to customize your system to meet your own particular needs. Items that can be regulated through the use of the Control Panel include: the look of your screen elements, fonts, keyboard and mouse responses, devices connected to your computer, time, date, language, and currency and measurements units.

To make changes to the settings in earlier versions of Windows, users would often need to edit the various .INI files that Windows used to set up the computer hardware and the Windows desktop. With Windows 3.1, most of these changes can be accomplished through the Control Panel. (Some changes may also be made through the Program Manager or File Manager.)

In this chapter, we will examine some of the Control Panel functions. The functions that will be covered are ones that can be easily "repaired" if you accidentally change/delete key default settings. You will not be asked to complete any actions that may significantly change the performance of Windows.

Starting Control Panel

The Control Panel icon is located in the Main window of the Program Manager. Complete the steps below to open the Control Panel window.

1 Open the Main window, inside the Program Manager window, then double-click on the Control Panel icon to start the Control Panel program.

2 Compare the Control Panel window on your screen with the window shown in Figure 10.1.

Figure 10.1 displays a typical Control Panel window. (See the table below for a list of all tool functions.) The look of the Control Panel window is determined by the hardware and software that you have configured to work with Windows. Therefore, the Control Panel appearing on your monitor may not exactly match the one in the illustration. The line of text at the bottom of the window lists the function of the selected tool.

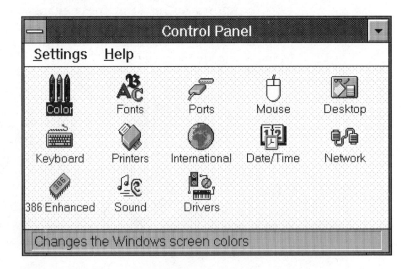

Figure 10.1 The Control Panel window.

Tool	Function
Color	Controls the color scheme of the desktop and most window elements.
Fonts	Allows for adding or removing fonts for the screen, printer, or plotter.
Ports	Allows for setting the default parameters for up to four serial ports.
Mouse	Allows for customizing the speed of the cursor moving across the screen, the double-click speed, and the functions of the left and right buttons. Also allows for a trail of the current mouse movements to be displayed.
Desktop	Changes the patterns or pictures used with the desktop and the screen saver; adjusts the cursor blink rate, window border widths, and icon spacing.
Keyboard	Adjusts the time setting for repeating keystrokes when keys are kept depressed.
Printers	Used for installing and removing printers, choosing the printer options, assigning output ports, and specifying the default printer.
International	Allows for selecting international settings, such as country, language, currency, time, date, and number formats. (Does not change the language of Windows, only the way programs use this information.)
Date/Time	Allows for setting the system date and time.
Network	Controls how Windows works on a network. This icon is displayed only when Windows is told it is to be used on a network.
386 Enhanced	Used for specifying how programs, concurrently running in the 386 mode, will work with the computer resources and peripheral devices. Also used for specifying the settings for swap files. This icon will appear only when Windows is operating in the 386 enhanced mode.
Sound	For computers equipped with a sound board and the properly installed driver, allows for assigning sound files (instead of the normal beep) to common computer events.

Tool	Function
Drivers	Used to install drivers for optional hardware devices, such as multimedia devices or digitized tablets.
MIDI Mapper (not shown in Figure 10.1)	Used to specify MIDI (Musical Instrument Digital Interface) setups for sound devices, such as a synthesizer.

To choose a Control Panel tool, double-click on its icon or choose the desired command from the SETTINGS menu.

Setting the Screen Element Colors with the Color Tool

When Windows is first installed, the Windows Default color scheme is used to specify the colors (or shades) for the various Windows screen elements, including the window frame, window background, active title bar, inactive title bar, etc. Along with the default setting, Windows provides a number of other predefined color schemes.

The Color tool enables you to choose one of the predefined color schemes, create your own color scheme, and (if desired) create your own colors.

In the following exercises, you will choose schemes from the list of predefined color schemes, create your own color scheme, and learn how to save your color schemes.

NOTE: In the following sections you will make some temporary modifications to the existing Windows color scheme, and you will learn how to add and delete color schemes from your desktop. As previously noted, the .INI files (normally located in your Windows directory) contain the various commands that allow you to control how Windows interacts with your computer. To protect yourself from losing color schemes (or other settings) that were deleted by mistake, you may want to copy your current .INI files onto your Data Disk before completing the exercises. This will provide a backup copy of your current settings. If you accidently remove settings that you need, just copy the .INI files on your Data Disk back into your Windows directory. Complete the following steps to place copies of your .INI files on your floppy disk.

1. Place your Data Disk in the appropriate drive.

2. Open the File Manager and select the directory that holds your Windows program.

3. Choose the FILE-Search... command to display the Search dialog box.

4. Enter *.INI in the text box (in the standard installation, the .INI files are located in the Windows directory) and choose the OK button.

5. The Search Results window should list the .INI files that Windows uses to set up your system.

6. Copy the .INI files onto your Data Disk.

7. Hopefully you will not need to use the backup copies of your files. However, upon completion of the exercises, if the wrong files were removed, you may copy the .INI files from your Data Disk into the Windows directory on your hard disk. This should enable you to run Windows as you did before starting the chapter.

When you complete the following exercise, you will have learned how to switch among the various color schemes available to you when you first load Windows.

1 Load the Color tool by double-clicking on its icon in the Control Panel Window. This action will cause the Color dialog box to appear (see Figure 10.2).

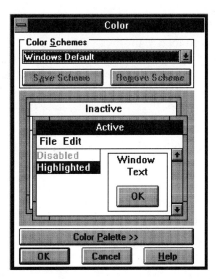

Figure 10.2 The Color dialog box.

2 Locate the Color Schemes frame (in the top portion of the dialog box) and record the name of the color scheme that is currently being used. (Windows Default is the name of the color scheme in Figure 10.2.) The current color scheme is _____.

Then click on the down arrow to expose the drop-down list box that displays the names of additional color schemes.

3 Utilize the scroll bar to scroll through the choices. Select the "Hotdog Stand" choice. The "sample screen," located in the middle of the dialog box, will immediately change to display the results of your choice.

4 Although you can repeat steps 2 and 3 to select and view other color schemes, a faster method is to press the up and down keyboard cursor keys. After each keystroke, the name of a color scheme appears in the Color Schemes box, and the sample screen will show what the screen elements look like for each choice.

View the remaining color schemes by pressing the up and down cursor keys. (When repeated presses of the same cursor key do not change the color scheme, you are at either the beginning or end of the list.)

5 Once you find a color scheme you like, apply the color scheme to your entire Windows environment by clicking on the OK button in the lower left corner of the dialog box. (Do not click on the OK button located in the Window Text frame.) This action also closes the Color tool and returns you to the Control Panel.

NOTE: The predefined color scheme you selected in the exercise above remains in effect until you change the color scheme again. If you are working at a standalone station, and you exit Windows (without changing the current color scheme), the next time you load Windows you will see the color scheme you have just chosen (instead of the one you used when you started this chapter). If you are working in a networked environment, the network administrator may have chosen a particular color scheme to initially load (for all users) each time Windows is started.

One of the most important aspects of Windows is its flexibility. If you are not satisfied with any of the color schemes you have seen, you may create your own color combinations. The next exercise demonstrates how to construct your own color scheme.

1 If necessary, open the Control Panel, choose the Color tool, and select the Window Default color scheme.

2 Click on the Color Palette button, to expand the Color dialog box to include the additional elements displayed in Figure 10.3.

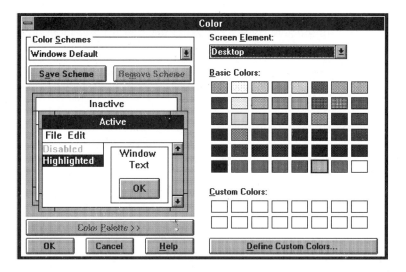

Figure 10.3 The expanded Color dialog box.

3 Select the menu bar element by either

   a. clicking on the menu bar in the sample screen section of the dialog box, or

   b. clicking on the down arrow next to the Screen Element box to expose the drop-down list box naming the screen elements. Then click on the menu bar choice.

4 Click on a number of the color boxes displayed in the Basic Colors section of the dialog box and view the changes to the menu bar in the sample box. (Depending on how your system is configured, some color choices may not appear in the sample box.)

   Choose a color for the menu bar by clicking on the desired color and then choosing the OK button in the lower-left corner of the dialog box.

5 Use a similar procedure to choose new colors for the remaining window elements.

6 (Optional step) Naming and saving your new color scheme allows you to switch between it and the predefined ones provided with Windows (or other ones that you have created). You save a new color scheme by:

   a. clicking on the Save Scheme button,

   b. entering the desired color scheme name in the text box of the Save Scheme dialog box,

c. clicking on OK in the Save Scheme dialog box. This step displays the name of the new color scheme in the Color Schemes text box of the Color dialog box.

   If you are using Windows on a network, you may not be able to save your color scheme. Check with your network administrator before saving any color schemes.

NOTE: A predefined color scheme may be removed by following the steps below. (A note of caution: Once a color scheme is removed, it is deleted from your Windows directory.)

1. Open the Control Panel.

2. Open the Color dialog box.

3. Open the Color Schemes list and select the color scheme to be deleted.

4. Click on the Remove Scheme button.

5. When the confirmation dialog box appears, choose Yes.

7 If you saved a color scheme in step 6, remove it now by following the steps listed above.

8 Return to the color scheme you started with at the beginning of this section.

Changing the Desktop

The Desktop dialog box is displayed by double-clicking on its icon in the Control Panel. Because you have already worked with the Control Panel Desktop module in Chapter 2, and you are familiar with obtaining more information about a Windows concept through using the various Help facilities, we will move ahead to some of the other Control Panel tools.

Working with Fonts

The font you choose to display your text has a tremendous impact on the appearance (and possibly, the effectiveness) of your document. Choose a font that is too small, and many people will not read your document because it is too hard to read. If your font is too large, potential readers may feel there are too many pages to read. Some fonts are very effective for showing short, bulleted lists, but hard to read if used in a longer document. As you work with

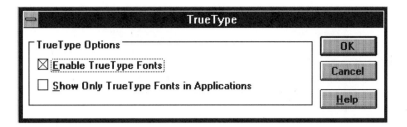

Figure 10.4 The TrueType dialog box.

the various fonts that come with the Windows package, you'll develop favorite fonts for particular situations. As you continue working with a computer, you will likely reach a point where you may want to add more fonts to your system.

Using TrueType Fonts

When your system uses TrueType fonts, it uses the same file to show the font on the screen that it uses to print the font on your paper. This helps make the printing process much more predictable. For this reason, some Windows users prefer to use only TrueType fonts.

You can use the Fonts tool to display only TrueType font options (for the programs you access through Windows) by completing the following steps:

1. Open the Fonts dialog box and click on the TrueType button to display the TrueType dialog box (see Figure 10.4).

2. Select the Show Only TrueType Fonts in Applications option (the default is Enable TrueType Fonts).

3. Click on the OK button.

Date and Time Settings

Changing the date and time settings was discussed previously in Chapter 6. Display the Date/Time dialog box by double-clicking on its icon in the Control Panel window and make the desired changes in the corresponding text boxes.

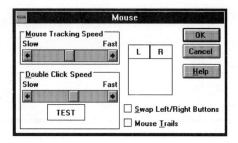

Figure 10.5   The Mouse dialog box.

Working with the Mouse Settings

You may customize your mouse actions by changing the settings displayed in the Mouse dialog box (see Figure 10.5). Display the Mouse dialog box by double-clicking on the Mouse icon in the Control Panel window.

To change the rate at which the pointer moves across the screen, drag the box in the Mouse Tracking Speed scroll bar to the left (slower) or right (faster).

To modify the speed with which Windows recognizes a "double-click," move the box in the Double Click Speed scroll bar to the left (slower) or right (faster). Check your new setting by clicking on the Test button and then double-clicking the mouse. If the box changes color, Windows received the double-click, if the box does not change colors, slide the box to the left and test the speed again.

To switch the functions of the left and right mouse buttons, select the Swap Left/Right Buttons option. When this option is selected, the functions are swapped immediately (before the dialog box is closed.)

The remaining check box is used to improve the visibility of the mouse pointer (by displaying a mouse trail) if you are using an LCD display adapter. (This option is dimmed if your display adapter does not support this function.)

Summary

The **Control Panel Color** and **Desktop Modules** play major roles in determining the appearance of your desktop; while the **Fonts tool** helps to control the appearance of the characters in your printed document. We first looked at the Desktop tool in Chapter 2, as the Desktop dialog box was used to explain many of the common dialog box controls and commands. As you learned how to work with dialog boxes, you were also learning to adjust your desktop to meet your needs.

The **Color tool** is used to color or shade the screen elements, such as the window borders, background, title bar, menu bar, text, etc. Windows provides a number of predefined color schemes and lets you create your own color schemes for the screen elements. If desired, you can even create your own colors.

The **Fonts tool** is used for viewing, adding, and removing fonts. It can also be used to display only TrueType font options for your Windows programs. The advantage of using TrueType fonts is that their printed appearance is virtually identical to their screen appearance.

The **Date/Time tool** enables you to set the system time and date.

The **Mouse tool** enables you to control the mouse tracking and double-click speed, swap the functions of the left and right button, and (if desired) leave a trail where the mouse has traveled.

Applications

After completing the reading and exercises included in the ten chapters of this text, you should now have a solid foundation from which to run your Windows program.

Your final assignment consists of two parts:

1. Use the Control Panel tools to customize the look and feel of your Windows package. If possible, save your settings.

2. Review the information in the text and identify any remaining questions you may have on any Windows topic. Refer to the Windows Help facility and manuals to try to answer these questions. If you cannot find all of the answers, turn in the remaining questions to your instructor.

Required Hardware,
Windows Installation,
Installing Windows, and
Non-Windows Software

Required Hardware

Windows 3.1 runs in either the *standard mode* or the *386 enhanced mode*. (The previous version, Windows 3.0, also had a "real" mode.) The standard mode is more restrictive, but it can be used with less powerful computers. Windows will automatically run in the standard mode in computers using an 80286 microprocessor. Windows may be run in either mode in computers using an 80386 or 80486 microprocessor.

The standard mode allows you to simultaneously run as many Windows-based applications as your computer's available memory allows (using conventional and extended memory). For many Windows applications, the standard mode runs faster than the 386 enhanced mode. You may also run DOS-based applications from the standard mode, but they must use the full screen. When running a DOS-based application, with Windows in the standard mode, all other applications are temporarily suspended.

The following *minimum* computer configuration is needed to run Windows in the *standard mode:* a computer with an 80286 processor (or higher); MS-DOS 3.1 (or later); 640 kilobytes (K) of conventional memory plus 256K of extended memory; 6 megabytes (MB) of free space on the hard disk; at least one floppy disk drive; and an EGA (or better) Windows-compatible graphics adapter and monitor.

Windows can also run in the 386 enhanced mode. This mode allows the user greater functionality but requires more powerful computing hardware. Running Windows in the 386 enhanced mode allows the user to conduct multitasking of non-Windows applications and enables the user to run these applications in full screen or inside resizable windows. The 386 enhanced mode provides the user with the virtual memory capabilities of the 386 and 486 processors; Windows can treat free space on the hard drive as extra memory. The computer then gains access to more memory than is physically available on the system (called virtual memory), and this speeds computer processing when the user is simultaneously running multiple tasks and applications.

The following *minimum* computer configuration is needed to run Windows in the *386 enhanced mode:* a computer with a 386SX processor (or higher); MS-DOS 3.1 (or later); 640K of conventional memory plus 1024K of extended memory; 8MB of free space on the hard disk; at least one floppy disk drive; and an EGA (or better) Windows-compatible graphics adapter and monitor.

Although not required, a Windows-compatible mouse, VGA (or SVGA) graphics adaptor and monitor, and a minimum of 4MB of RAM are highly recommended to provide a more satisfying performance from Windows. In addition, installing a Windows-compatible modem and using the Windows communication accessory (Terminal) provides the means for connecting to various computer bulletin boards, networks, and database services.

Installing Windows

Installing Windows 3.1 is quite easy. There are two methods for installing Windows 3.1, Express Setup or Custom Setup. The *Express* Setup procedure automatically identifies your hardware and existing software and modifies key Windows files to work with your system. The only technical questions asked in Express Setup are where to store the Windows files, the type of printer being used, and the port the printer is connected to. Most users should choose the Express option.

While the *Custom* Setup option gives a user greater control over how Windows is installed in his or her system, it is recommended that only experienced computer users choose the Custom Setup option. The range of questions asked of the user during Custom Setup involve: the name of the directory used to store the Windows files; type of computer, monitor, mouse, and printer; printer port(s) to be used; keyboard layout; language being used; which programs, already on the hard disk, are to be accessed from within Windows; changes to AUTOEXEC.BAT and CONFIG.SYS files; optional components of Windows to be installed; and the virtual-memory settings.

To install Windows on your C: drive (your hard drive), insert the first Windows disk in your floppy disk drive and enter the drive name and **setup** at the DOS prompt (i.e., enter **a:setup** at the C:\> prompt). After entering the setup command, follow the instructions on your monitor.

No matter which option you choose, the installation process should take no longer than 15–30 minutes. If at any time during the installation process you need to stop the procedure, press F3.

Installing Windows Applications

Once Windows is installed, you may install other applications designed to run within Windows (i.e., Microsoft Word for Windows. Windows applications utilize the same type of drop-down menus, dialog boxes, and icons as those used in Windows.

The standard method for installing a Windows application is listed below:

1. Display the Windows Program Manager or File Manager.

2. Open the FILE menu and choose the Run command.

3. Insert the disk that contains the application's setup or install program in your floppy drive and enter the name of the drive and the appropriate setup command (typically either **a:setup** or **a:install**) in the Run dialog box.

4. Follow the installation instructions displayed on your desktop.

Once the installation is completed, Windows provides an icon for the application and places it either in a separate group window created for the application, or in the Program Manager's Application group window.

Installing Non-Windows Applications

Install non-Windows applications from the DOS prompt. Use the installation procedure described in the application's manual.

To efficiently run a non-Windows application through Windows, Windows needs to work with a special program information file (PIF) designed for the non-Windows program. The PIF provides information (i.e., memory requirements) that Windows needs to manage the software. When Windows is installed, a number of PIFs are transferred to your Windows directory. The various PIFs are written to correspond with the most commonly used DOS applications. A default PIF is also copied to your Windows directory during the installation process. Generally, if a specific PIF is not available for your non-Windows application, the default PIF will provide sufficient information to allow Windows to run the software. You may create your own PIFs by using the PIF Editor found in the Main window in Program Manager. (See your Windows manual and the on-line Help facility for more information on the PIF Editor.)

If you installed a new program from the DOS prompt, after Windows was installed on your system, you may create a program-item icon for it by using the Program Manager FILE-New... command. However, for common DOS applications, you may benefit by using the Windows Setup utility found in the Program Manager Main window instead. Use of this utility creates a program-item icon and creates a PIF for the program in the Windows directory. Follow the steps below to use the Windows Setup utility.

1. Display the Program Manager Main window and double-click on the Windows Setup icon to display the Windows Setup window.

2. Open the (Windows Setup) OPTIONS menu and choose the Set Up Applications... command.

3. When the dialog box appears, indicate that you either want Windows to search the hard disk for various applications or that you will specify an application. (If you are only adding the new application, you may prefer to choose the second option.) Then choose OK.

4. If you chose to specify the application, you must list the path and the desired program's startup command in the Setup Applications dialog box that is now appearing on the desktop. (Or you may choose the Browse button to find the startup file.)

   By default, an icon for the program will be placed in Program Manager's Application window; you may select a different window from the Add to Program Group drop-down list box in the dialog box.
   Then choose OK.

5. Windows then searches for the corresponding PIF. If a specific PIF exists for the program, it is matched with the program. Windows then displays a dialog box asking you to select/confirm the name of the program. For some applications, a list of possible program names will be displayed. Select the appropriate name from the list, then choose the OK button to confirm the name.

   Completion of this step causes the program to be set up to work with Windows, and a program-item icon will be displayed in the selected group window.

═══ **Appendix B** ═══

Print Manager

Print Manager is a utility that manages the printing for all Windows-based applications. When you choose the Print command from the FILE menu of a Windows application, the application sends the print file to the Print Manager. While Print Manager controls the printing process, your application is available to work on other projects.

Print Manager runs in the background and is available to receive print jobs from any Windows application. When you are running your program in a non-maximized window, you may see the Print Manager icon in the lower part of your desktop when it works with your file. If the lower part of your desktop is covered by a window, the Print Manager icon will be not be visible. In this case, you may open Task List to see that the Print Manager program is open. Print Manager closes automatically once the file is completely sent to the printer and there are no printing problems.

If numerous files are sent to the Print Manager, the files are placed in a "print queue," which is a list of files waiting to be printed. The list is established in the order that Print Manager received the print requests. Print Manager can create two types of queues: a network print queue (which services the computers sharing a network printer) and a local queue (which lists the files to be printed by the printer attached to your computer).

Double-clicking on the Print Manager icon in the Program Manager Main window, or double-clicking on the Print Manager icon that appears near the bottom of the desktop when a Print command has been given, opens the Print Manager window. Figure B.1 displays the Print Manager window.

Although the window work area may display information from a number of print queues, only one queue appears in Figure B.1. The top line in the work area is a printer information line that lists the name of the printer and the port in use. Located below the printer information line is the file information line, which lists the file(s) currently in the queue (in this example, the CH7PRAC.WRI file, created in the Write accessory), the percentage of the file

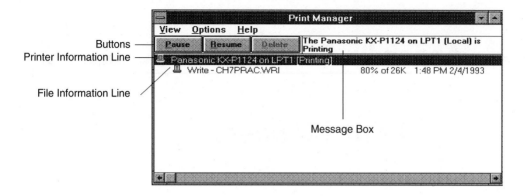

Buttons
Printer Information Line

File Information Line

Message Box

Figure B.1 The Print Manager window.

already printed when the window is viewed, the size of the file, and the time and date of the print request.

When more than one print request is listed, each request is numbered, and the numbered files appear (in order) below the corresponding printer information line. Because the lower-numbered files were sent first, they are located near the top of the queue and will be printed before the higher-numbered files. After a print job has been sent to the printer, the corresponding file information line is removed from the window.

There may be times when it is beneficial to change the order of the files in the queue. To modify the queue, simply drag a file to the desired location in the list and release the mouse button. After moving a file to a new position within the queue, the files are automatically renumbered to reflect their new order.

Print Manager Buttons

Located between the Print Manager menu and work area are three buttons (Pause, Resume, and Delete) and a message area that Print Manager uses to display any pertinent printing messages.

To temporarily stop the printer, click on the Pause button. If you are using more than one printer, you must first select the appropriate printer—just move the pointer to the desired printer information line and click the left mouse button. A common reason to choose the Pause button is seeing that your printer is running low on paper. To re-start the printer, choose the Resume button.

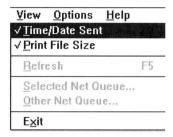

Figure B.2 The Print Manager VIEW menu.

If you have sent a file to the Print Manager, but decide it is not necessary to print the file, open the Print Manager window and locate the file in the print queue. Select the appropriate file information line (the selected line appears in reverse video) and choose the Delete button. A dialog box will then appear asking you to confirm the deletion. Deleting a file from the print queue does not affect the file stored on your disk or in the computer memory.

The Print Manager Menu

The VIEW menu (see Figure B.2) allows you to display various information in the file information line, work with network printers, and exit the Print Manager window.

The commands at the top of the VIEW menu provide the option of displaying the Time/Date Sent and Print File size in the file information lines. (The default setting displays these options.) To turn an option off, open the VIEW menu and click on the option. (This will also remove the checkmark located in front of the option name.)

For computers connected to a network printer, the Refresh, Select Net Queue... and Other Net Queue... commands allow you to monitor the operations of your network printer(s).

Selecting the VIEW-Exit command closes the Print Manager window. (Remember, even when the window is closed, Print Manager is available whenever a Windows Print command is given.)

The OPTIONS menu (see Figure B.3) lets you adjust the speed in which Print Manager sends data to the printer port, choose how Print Manager reports problems, control your network printer settings and connections, and set up your local printer.

Figure B.3 The Print Manager OPTIONS menu.

To change the amount of processor time Print Manager receives, in comparison to your other applications, select one of the "priority" options located in the top section of this menu.

High priority: assigns more computer resources to the Print Manager, which results in your other applications running more slowly.

Medium priority (the default setting): attempts to evenly distribute the resources between Print Manager and the applications that are running.

Low priority: gives more resources to the applications that are running—the applications run faster, but Print Manager slows down.

The OPTIONS menu provides three choices for displaying Print Manager messages:

Alert Always: enables Print Manager (even when minimized) to display an error message dialog box.

Flash if Inactive (the default setting): causes the Print Manager Icon to flash when an error occurs; or if the Print Manager window is open but not active, the window title bar will flash. Opening the flashing icon, or making the window active, allows Print Manager to display the error message.

Ignore if Inactive: will indicate error messages only when the Print Manager window is open and active.

Dragging Files from the File Manager to the Print Manager Icon

You may print files directly from the File Manager window by dragging associated file icons, from the directory windows, onto the minimized Print Manager icon or open Print Manager window. For example, if the File Manager directory window is displaying the CH7PRAC.WRI file, and the Print Manager window is open on your desktop (or the minimized Print Manager icon is displayed), you need only click on the CH7PRAC.WRI file icon and drag it on top of either the Print Manager window or minimized icon to initiate the printing process. Because the .WRI extension is associated with the Write accessory, a Write window dialog box opens to indicate that the file is being prepared to be printed.

Index